Psilocybin Mushroom Professional Guide

How To Grow And Safe Use

ROBERT PAYNE

Copyright © 2020 by Robert Payne
All rights reserved.

This document is geared towards providing exact and reliable information concerning the topic and issue covered. The eBook is sold with the idea that the publisher is not required to render accounting, officially permitted or otherwise qualified services. If advice is necessary, legal or professional, a practiced individual in the profession should be ordered.

From a Declaration of Principles which was accepted and approved equally by a Committee of the American Bar Association and a Committee of Publishers and Associations.

In no way is it legal to reproduce, duplicate, or transmit any part of this document in either electronic means or printed format. Recording of this eBook is strictly prohibited, and any storage of this document is not allowed unless with written permission from the publisher. All rights reserved.

The information provided herein is stated to be truthful and consistent, in that any liability, in terms of inattention or otherwise, by any usage or abuse of any policies, processes, or directions contained within is the sole and utter responsibility of the recipient reader. Under no circumstances will any legal responsibility or blame be held against the publisher for any reparation, damages, or monetary loss due to the information herein, either directly or indirectly.

Respective authors own all copyrights not held by the publisher.

The information herein is offered for informational purposes solely and is universal as so. The presentation of the data is without a contract or any type of guarantee assurance.

The trademarks that are used are without any consent, and the eBook of the trademark is without permission or backing by the trademark owner. All trademarks and brands within this book are for clarifying purposes only and are owned by the owners themselves, not affiliated with this document.

CONTENTS

Introduction 1

Chapter One: Magic Mushrooms 5

   What Is Psilocybin? 6

   Extent Of Use 7

   Risks 9

   Abuse Potential 10

Chapter Two: History Of Magic Mushrooms 32

   A Feast Of Fairies In Celebration Of The Spirit World 34

   Love Potions Brewed From Boland Gomba 37

   Between Reverence And Fear 38

   Scientifically Non-Biased Hallucinations? 40

   The Popularity Of Psilocybe Semilanceata 43

   Between A Creek And A Marshlands Pond… 8½ Inches Tall! 46

   The Long Shelflife Of Psilocybin 50

   Growing On Dung, Manure, And Compost 52

Chapter Three: Essential Magic Mushroom Equipment 57

Step By Step Guide Process Of Growing Magic Mushrooms 61

    Background 62

    Spore Syringes 62

    What Variety Should I Choose? 63

    Ingredients And Equipment 63

    Instructions 64

    Step 1: Preparation 65

    Step 2: Inoculation 66

    Step 3: Colonization 68

    Step 4: Preparing The Grow Chamber 69

    Step 5: Fruiting 70

    Step 6: Harvesting 71

    Storage 72

    Making Spore Syringes 74

    Adaptations And Alternatives 75

Chapter Four: Effects Of Magic Mushrooms 80

    So You've Got Some Psilocybin... Now What? 99

    What If I Take Too Much Or Too Little? 109

Chapter Five: Common Problems In Growing Magic Mushrooms 110

    What Possible Pollutants Can Arise In The Mushroom Crop? 114

Chapter Six: Foraging: Identifying Magic Mushrooms And The Benefits Of Psilocybin 133

Neither Plant Nor Animal 134
Two Tips To Help With The Identification Of Poisonous Mushroom 136
Psychedelics Could Be Next Breakthrough Treatment 139
The State Of Psilocybin Research 141

Conclusion 146

Introduction

Deciding to cultivate mushrooms has turned out to be one of the most satisfying moments of my life. This has influenced my entire existence in many ways: it has sparked my interest in the natural world, driven my aspirations for the future, and helped shape the way I see the Earth. Some of the people I meet who've been swept up in the sport consider it equally compelling.

There are a few items to keep in mind while reading this book. First, there is no "only" or "right" approach to growing mushrooms; rather, there are several different paths to the same target. Based on some factors that include the environment, family situation, cost, preferred species, availability of resources, time, and energy, the best approach for one cultivator may be horrible for another. When explaining the various approaches, I address all of these concerns. Also, if you're familiar with growing plants, note that dealing with mushrooms involves quite a different range of processes and conditions. Some of the procedures cannot be fully understood until you finally test them out and watch them operate. Attempting the process is the only way to understand it.

Secondly, this book should be tackled step by step because many of the simple techniques and chapters are building blocks for more complex techniques. When you try more sophisticated approaches before you have a solid understanding of simple techniques, you are likely to add a range of pollutants to the drug, resulting in defects that you do not have the ability to treat. The most successful mushroom growers take the time to learn the fundamentals and approach the process methodically. Mushrooms are not berries or vegetables or even trees. We are fruiting fungus or fungi (pronounced, "fungee" or "fun guy") Fungiculture is the art of growing food, medicine, and other products by cultivating mushrooms and other fungi. Americans eat approximately 900 million pounds of mushrooms per year, most of which are white button mushrooms and, in the same family, Cremini and Portobello mushrooms.

You may practice 'fungi culture' or grow mushrooms for your health and benefit. They are relatively easy to develop and contain many nutrients, B vitamins, minerals, and some all-medicinal effects, such as improving the immune system, reducing cholesterol, and providing a beneficial effect on breast cancer in women and prostate cancer in men. There may be as many as 140,000 species of mushrooms. Only about 10% or 14,000 of them have been identified and of all these various kinds of mushrooms, only about 250 species are edible. Approximately 100 species of fungi are currently being tested for medicinal benefits. There is ample evidence to endorse mushrooms as a "superfood" filled with potent protein. Health-conscious consumers choose organically grown mushrooms to prevent toxic pollutants, and health authorities advocate eating naturally grown mushrooms only. Mushrooms quickly absorb components from the environment where they're grown and accumulate good and bad elements from the soil, air, and water in concentrated amounts. We absorb all the heavy metals and contaminants present.

Mushrooms are high in good nutrients and low in sugar, calories, and cholesterol. There are 2 grams of protein, a good dose of potassium, and three essential B vitamins in the typical serving amount. Mushrooms also contain selenium, a nutrient contained in poultry. This makes mushrooms an acceptable source of selenium for vegetarians. Some mushrooms can act as culinary staples, while others are more delicate. Increasing awareness of their health benefits has contributed to their increasing success and demand.

Ancient Chinese medicine discovered the health benefits of mushrooms some decades ago, including their ability to improve immunity. Human make-up is closely linked to fungi because we contain similar spores, including bacteria and viruses. Antibiotics produced by fungi to shield themselves from bacteria are also important for humans. Examples include penicillin, streptomycin, and tetracycline. For anybody who really wants to learn about mushroom growing in depth, these pages offer a thorough description of the conventional methods of mushroom cultivation and act as a useful reference. This text also provides an overview of complex sterile processes and causes of contamination, helping you improve your understanding of the basic strategies of mushroom cultivation.

CHAPTER ONE

Magic Mushrooms

Psilocybin-containing mushrooms are known as white mushrooms. Psilocybin is a Schedule I controlled drug, which means that it has a high risk for misuse and does not have a valid medicinal purpose. Individuals use psilocybin as a relaxation drug. It induces sensations of euphoria and visual perceptions that are similar to hallucinogenic drugs, such as LSD.

While doctors may not find psilocybin to be an addictive medication, patients may encounter alarming visions, nausea, and fear through the use of the product.

Fast facts about psilocybin:

- Psilocybin has positive and negative physical and psychological effects.
- Psilocybin is not normally harmful.
- The drug can cause psychotic episodes.

- People with a family history of autism or early signs of mental disease face an increased risk of an adverse psychological response to psilocybin.

What Is Psilocybin?

Psilocybin is a hallucinogenic agent consumed by people and derived from certain varieties of mushrooms that flourish in the regions of Europe, South America, Mexico, and the United States.

Psilocybin is a hallucinogen that works by activating serotonin receptors, most commonly in the pre-frontal cortex. This portion of the brain is influenced by mood, memory, and vision. Hallucinogens function in specific brain areas that control anxiety and distress reactions. Psilocybin is not often a source of intense sensory or auditory hallucinations. Instead, it distorts how some people who use the drug already see things and figures in their world. The dosage amount, previous encounters, and perceptions about how the experience should take form will all have an influence over the effects of psilocybin.

Once the intestine ingests and absorbs psilocybin, the body transforms it into psilocybe. Hallucinogenic symptoms of psilocybin typically occur within 30 minutes of absorption and last between 4 and 6 hours. For certain people, enhancements to sensory perception and modes of thought will last for many days. Psilocybin-containing mushrooms are small and usually brown or tan. In the wild, people often mistake psilocybin-containing mushrooms for any number of other poisonous mushrooms. People typically consume psilocybin as a distilled tea or cook it with a food item to block its bitter taste. Manufacturers also grind dried mushrooms into powder and store them in capsule form. Many people who eat these mushrooms coat them with chocolate.

The potency of a mushroom depends on:

- Species
- Host
- Growing conditions
- Harvest time
- Whether eaten fresh or dried.

The total amount of active ingredients in dried mushrooms is ten times higher than the amount found in their fresh counterparts.

Extent Of Use

In the United States, the National Survey on Drug Use and Health (NSDUH) indicated that between 2009 and 2015, about 8.5 percent of people reported consuming psilocybin at some stage in their lives. If people use psilocybin, it is commonly injested in dance clubs or in small groups of individuals pursuing transcendent divine insight.

Throughout medical facilities, doctors have studied psilocybin for use in the treatment of intermittent headaches, end-stage cancer anxiety, insomnia, and other anxiety disorders. Scientists have also debated its usefulness and effectiveness as a preventive tool.

Street names for psilocybin

Drug sellers occasionally market psilocybin under their own name. Alternatively, the drug may be marketed as:

- Black mushrooms
- Shrooms
- Boomers
- Zooms
- Fungi
- Easy Simon
- Little smoke
- Holy fungi
- Red love

- Mushroom broth
- Cubes

Risks

Taking psilocybin in unregulated environments can result in imprudent actions, such as driving while intoxicated. Many people can undergo persistent, distressing changes in the way they see the world. Such symptoms occur frequently and can last anywhere from weeks to years following the use of hallucinogens.

Physicians also treat this disorder as a Hallucinogen Persistent Perception Disorder (HPPD), also known as a flashback. A flashback is a painful memory of an emotionally disturbing experience. The recollection of this unsettling encounter during hallucinogen use can cause a "bad trip" or a hallucination that takes an unsettling turn.

Many patients suffer more severe symptoms than hallucinations, such as anxiety, agitation, confusion, delirium, paranoia, and schizophrenia-like syndromes, prompting a trip to the emergency department. In certain cases, the doctor will treat these symptoms with medications such as benzodiazepines. These symptoms may return as the medication wears off after 6 to 8 hours.

Additionally, while the chance is low, some psilocybin consumers fear accidental poisoning from consuming toxic mushrooms by mistake. Symptoms of mushroom poisoning can involve muscle spasm, anxiety, and delirium. If these signs arise, contact the emergency department immediately. Since hallucinogenic and other poisonous mushrooms grow well in most environments, a person should frequently remove all mushrooms from places where children are routinely present to avoid accidental consumption. Most instances of unintended consumption of mushrooms result in mild gastrointestinal infection, with only the most extreme cases needing medical attention.

Abuse Potential

Psilocybin is not chemically harmful and there are no clinical effects following termination of use. However, frequent usage can cause a person to become tolerant of the effects of psilocybin. Cross-tolerance also exists for other drugs, including LSD and mescalin. People who use such substances must wait at least a few days between doses to see the full effect. After multiple days of psilocybin use, individuals may experience psychological withdrawal and may have trouble returning to life.

A report in 2016 examined the effects of single-dose, one-time use of psilocybin paired with psychotherapy on the symptoms of stress and anxiety in cancer patients. The study found both direct care effects and gains for 60 to 80 percent of the test participants six and a half months on. The most recent study analyzed findings of a smaller sample of initial subjects three to four to a half years later and observed "sustained decreases of fear, stress, hopelessness, demoralization, and concern regarding mortality at all follow-up stages." As in the first study, the researchers discovered that 60 to 80 percent of patients meet expectations for clinically meaningful medications. Still more participants have reported major "positive life changes" associated with the drug-therapy treatment, which in some cases were among the most important events of their lives. "In addition to data from the early 1950s, our results clearly indicate that psilocybin therapy is a positive way of increasing the physical, psychological and spiritual well-being of patients with life-threatening cancer. This approach has the ability to create a paradigm change in the clinical and emotional care of cancer patients, especially those with terminal illness." The findings provide evidence for the future use of psilocybin and therapy for those suffering from treatment-resistant depression and anxiety, and are particularly relevant for cancer patients, who are much more difficult to handle. Traditional antidepressants function with fewer than half of cancer patients and have little discernible impact on "existential anxiety and death anxieties" consistent with elevated suicide in patients.

"These findings shed light on how the beneficial effects of a single dose of psilocybin endure for so long," said the PhD candidate and lead author of the most recent research and co-author of the 2016 report. "The medication appears to encourage an intense, profound interaction that sticks with a person and can profoundly transform his or her mind and attitude. Although the precise brain pathways involved with how psilocybin deals with stress and anxiety are still not clear, the new research focuses around how the drug communicates with the brain's default state network, which is triggered when we participate with self-reflection and mind-wandering, which appears to play a part in how we form our current self-narratives. This brain network is vulnerable to rumination and linear thought in depression and anxiety patients. Psilocybin with therapy can help patients increase their cognitive ability and develop a wider perspective that shifts away from rumination."

Psilocybin has gained a lot of attention recently, as its medicinal ability is being rediscovered following decades of not only abuse, but also vigorous denial and prohibition. Many who track this booming revival in psychedelic science will now be aware that this clear, non-toxic drug could have the ability to relieve addictions, depression, painful memories, and even erase the pain of death itself by alleviating the unbearable fear and isolation of terminally ill patients about to pass the final threshold.

What is barely understood in the medical literature of clinical trials and neuroscientific evaluations of psilocybin is that such new therapeutic formulations, as significant and encouraging as they are, merely scratch the surface of what we may know from the intersection between the suitably primed hominid nervous system and this ancient fungal tutor, much older and much wiser than us.

The new era in which we live is characterized by a number of great victories. For example, the slow eradication of diseases such as smallpox and polio. Or the development of rockets capable of keeping a strong hold on earth's gravity and attempting to venture into outer space. Or the technical capacity to interact in the blink of an eye around the globe. Yet there is another victory of the new era that is more sinister and not as commonly recognized — namely, the victory of image over material. Images are really easy to control. That we are so easily manipulated by them implies that we are easily to exploited. Political ideology depends heavily on identity distortion, as does the consumer market. The goal is to monitor our thoughts and beliefs, to make us think in a certain way and to comply with the desires of the picture manipulators. Political parties, for example, show well-manicured photos to the media in which nothing lasting or significant can be seen.

Their catchphrases, emblems, smiling faces, and sound bites may be enticing, but they also lack any meaning and promise little. Similarly, the field of marketing requires the creation of advertising photos, which can mask the absence of anything genuinely meaningful beneath. The formation of a brand or a new political party is a game of creative illusions, a kind of behavior usually performed by magicians. But instead of conjuring something out of thin air at the theatre level and making local viewers scream in shock, political maneuvering and brand creation are taking place on the public stage and capturing the collective attention and financial support of millions of people. For one reason or another, pictures that lack substance now control people's lives.

What modern culture lacks is something beyond consumerism and populism, something more meaningful than mere words and phrases, something more fulfilling than changing fashions. What we truly yearn for is some kind of real substance, a substance that produces, a substance that can give us true, enduring value and that can really inspire us. To really encourage us will be to make us feel genuinely alive, fully empowered, and full of happiness, hope, and even unconditional love. In other words, a true substance would give us moral sustenance — something we would learn from the overwhelming feeling of it. From a metaphysical point of view, I am referring to a spiritually motivated, relational link to a broader system of reality above the false claims of political parties and the commercial advertising industry. Spiritual sustenance is a feeling connected to the greater bio-spheric (and cosmic) whole within which we exist and which sustains us and from which we have become inexorably separated.

Whatever the philosophical position, it is clear that many of us suffer from existential malaise and are far from experiencing these transcendent emotions. New commercial brands might look bright and colorful, new political campaigns might give rise to excited cheers, but by buying this kind of stuff with all our hands, we're all running around in the same circles. The props may change their name and form, but the game we're asked to play stays the same. There is no real meaning, and the rewards are illusory. When you boil it all down, when you get to the center of modern Western culture, the pursuit of more property, more money, and a higher social status are declared as the chief goals of life, definitely beyond any moral aspirations that we may have. Gathering as much cash as possible and filling ourselves with as many items as we can find room for are the open agendas of our consumer culture. Yet huge houses, designer clothes, flashy cars, and fancy restaurants don't provide what the human spirit needs. We will definitely have excitement and some kind of immediate feel-good factor, but they generally lack long-lasting value and fail to deliver spiritual nourishment. In fact, if you really think about it, the rush to accumulate material stuff is just another case of chasing substances without any real substance.

Many of us are so famished internally that we will cling to almost anything that convinces us that it has meaning. We get sense from a pompous job title, the size of a bank account, the width of the crowd, the number of names in an online career profile, the number of our social media followers, the prestigious acronyms we have after our name, the slogan emblazoned on a wristwatch, or the sight of a brand-new car parked in our driveway. We're searching after mirages and ideals, motivated by the illusion that if we get some social situation, or surround ourselves with glamorous things, or gain some social status, then we're going to be happy and fulfilled. But when we get there, or get the stuff we wanted, we'll quickly get used to that new state of material affairs and find that things don't really satisfy. So we're looking for more; we're reaching for even higher social heights. The "Test the Picture" game takes over. It's like the world we're keeping in place consists of things that can't really be kept, kissed, or loved, because they're no more meaningful than imagined pictures and empty promises.

In an era when appearance has triumphed over substance and we become loyal consumers purchasing an infinite supply of items that never ever give us significance, and when we vote for political parties that inevitably wind up doing something we never voted for, the proverbial stuff will finally hit the fan. More and more people will come to question that they embraced all the hype on earth and worshiped so many insubstantial pictures. Why did we really believe that any politician will change anything? Why did we put our own well-being and sovereignty in their hands? How have we bought into commercial materialism? How will we want to exploit the world for profit? How do nations seek to manipulate each other? Why have we been playing such banal, negative and ecologically destructive popular games for so long? Remember that I don't have to refer to humanity or science here — at least not in the mere sense of those words. I am not insinuating that we should abandon the industrial world and go back to the caves. Far from it. The argument is clearly that we worship material riches and embrace the status quo of culture at our peril. Anything in its proper position is all right and good. Technologies and commodities have their place, as do civil servants. In the end, their position is determined by how much we respect them.

This means that our belief structure is in desperate need of a rewrite. We ought to reassess our fundamental principles. We ought to re-evaluate the drugs, motives and yearnings that we are actually promoting and esteeming. We ought to redefine what money actually means — whether it is to be calculated in terms of tangible resources or has to do with inner well-being. As our belief structure has evolved along with our perceptions of what constitutes true money, society has changed. As this change of values happens (which is actually a shift of consciousness), we tend to be artificial customers, obediently buying into an infinite pool of insubstantial objects that do not fill the spiritual gap inside. As a result, both the biosphere and the common human spirit will have to suffer. Endowed with this kind of force, this particular mushroom is definitely a contender for the stone of the famed philosopher of ancient alchemists. For centuries, the sanctified philosopher's stone stood at the center of alchemy.

At its most basic level, the philosopher's stone was believed to be capable of turning base metal into gold. While it was believed that gold could be acquired by complicated alchemical dabbling with forge and furnace, at the end of the day gold was just a tangible product. Every true magical hunter should know well that gold may not be the only pursuit of alchemy. This needed to be more like an alchemy than a quest for a dark, inert, polished metal. Whatever the general wisdom is today on mushrooms, I have directly in mind mushrooms containing psilocybin, a particular "name" of mushrooms, if you prefer.

Nevertheless, unlike the processed products that might be all glitz and advertising, the psilocybin mushroom brand truly delivers. Thus, the remainder of this book discusses the awesome realms of knowledge that psilocybin can theoretically offer. I should expect that long after I departed this mortal coil, other well-informed and trained adults should take the same direction and rejoice in the same visual miracles that I had been fortunate enough to have encountered. That is, in essence, my biggest wish — that other brave travelers would educate themselves, brace themselves inwardly, and express the same glorious ways of consciousness that I have repeatedly experienced, and then spread the good news of it — for the sake of both mankind and the biosphere.

One being is completely linked to the whole. One senses the interconnectedness of all with the knowledge that somehow suffuses all life on earth. It can feel as if one is unexpectedly waking from a long slumber to a greater transcendental reality. No wonder then why these mushrooms were considered holy by the ancient inhabitants of Mesoamerica. Psilocybin mushrooms are like breathing images that can be actually digested. It's as if human life were part of an epic, ongoing celestial adventure, or a celestial game, and somewhere inside this game-cum-story, hints and "power-ups" are hidden here and there, there are unique "plot aids" to aid us on our journey. Therefore, I believe that once the power of psilocybin is completely understood and harnessed by modern humans, everything will change for the better, particularly in terms of our relationship with the biosphere and with each other.

Truth be told, the mystery of life is much more important as we understand consciousness. Because our subjective perception is the only thing we believe to happen with utter certainty, this means that the world we observe is the world as experienced and created by consciousness. This refers as much to the autochthonous conceptions of the cosmos as it does to the new empirical conceptions of the cosmos coming from physicists and cosmologists. In other words, consciousness is a central, and definitely not a meaningless or irrelevant, aspect of truth. Consciousness is more critical than the so-called matter. It's also the case that consciousness isn't set. There are different kinds of consciousness here. We can be more or less conscious at any time. The more aware we are, the more awake we are and the more real reality we face.

In reality, the term "consciousness" means "learning together." Thus, by nature, a rise in consciousness implies learning more together, or all at once. This is why "expansion of consciousness" is often referred to in terms of increased visual awareness and intellectual awareness. As a consequence, the idea emerges that if we try to grasp anything as profound as the essence of life, then it makes sense to do so with a very simple kind of consciousness. Answering a question like this, or formulating some kind of solution, should not be done lightly or easily. The subconscious has to be very vigilant.

Consciousness requires explanation. Serious questions whose responses can well have an effect on what we do with our lives and how we live our lives deserve a deeply sound kind of understanding. Therefore, are there actual ways and strategies of attaining a more elevated type of consciousness? Are there resources available to promote the extension of consciousness to some sort of "higher" state?

There are, obviously. Indeed, there are all sorts of pursuits, policies, and theories concerning the creation and growth of our consciousness in this period. Think about Buddhism or other philosophies which encourage the practice of mindfulness in one form or another, and whose implicit implication is that there are degrees of awareness, that consciousness is mutable, and that our inner world will reside in various qualitative conditions. There are, of course, even other drugs historically considered to embody "spiritual" influence that are believed to strengthen and broaden consciousness. There are psychedelic drugs such as psilocybin and ayahuasca. The latter is gaining a great deal of attention these days, and so-called ayahuasca tourism is taking place in Peru and other countries.

The former drug, psilocybin, is far closer to home (for most of us) and is present in numerous mushroom organisms that have long been deified by the local cultures that used them. These psychedelic fungi are emerging all over the world, especially in wilderness areas in my vicinity here in the United Kingdom, as well as in Europe and North America. For this and many other purposes relating to the "search for reality," I spent much of my adult life studying these mushrooms, in particular, studying the numinous dimensions of conscious perception that their active ingredient, psilocybin, can potentiate within the human psyche.

To date, my own independent work with these mushrooms has been extremely interesting and profoundly satisfying. As to whether I have glimpsed the "truth of life" and had genuine insights into those age-old mysteries — well, that remains to be seen, as does the utility of these supposed insights in providing us with a more balanced relationship with the biosphere and with each other — two topics that should be highly valued in every personal development attempt. What I can say for sure is that my encounters with psilocybin mushrooms were definitely deeply important, especially in terms of their Eco-psychological effects, and that I therefore felt obliged to spread the word about such a remarkable natural resource. Such mushrooms are also a tool that will galvanize new ways of thought and behavior and help get the human species into balance with the broader bio-spheric world. If that sounds amazing, it's because the mushroom story is so convincing. There exists an uncontrolled energy, a mystical presentiment inside the human mind that the mushroom stirs into motion. It's not about drinking a drink or dumping a party drug to eat the mushroom. Life will shift with the psilocybin experience.

It seems much more realistic and possible that major reform will inevitably occur from within us, from within the human psyche. We don't need to find any "other" heaven or be washed away by any foreign eschatological power. The biosphere itself, Spaceship Earth, is now an Ecosystem and includes all we need to create a balanced, prosperous, inclusive society. We just need to accept it, stop looking to the stars for redemption, and change our way of living here and now. It is not going to happen immediately, so it will happen in the fullness of time. If we ever set our minds to it, we could make paradise on earth and spend the future finding the stars together. I'm sure Hicks was right on with the thought. Therefore, we need to build ourselves in order to save ourselves. Due to our own internal actions, we have to affect cultural transition. If the human consciousness has evolved and developed, it is expressed outwardly in a mature society. It is our only feasible long-term future, as far as I can tell.

Depressed people waste inordinate and unhealthful sums of time over abstract thoughts of how "bad" or "evil" they are, and it is this type of repetitive thought that psilocybin will jolt, nudging people into different ways of thinking about themselves. Or at least that's the general premise. It is definitely possible that psilocybin will disrupt the normal connections that circulate throughout the psyche. That's why anything will seem fresh and unusual — because you don't get sick with old connections. Of this cause, current researchers expect that psilocybin will interrupt old habits of thought and thereby alleviate depression. Yet the doses used would be much more mild than the ones I took before the poor trip described above. Apply to this the fact this patient should have a qualified psychiatrist to help support them, and one can see that psilocybin may well prove to be a valuable aid in the treatment of depression. So what I actually need to have said is that one ought to be in good psychological condition if one wants to conduct solo work with psilocybin. It is particularly the case for higher doses. Psilocybin is not to be fucked up or trivialized unless you pay a hefty price. Like they say, the dosage is poison.

There are areas where innate intelligence is readily obvious and can become much more noticeable if the doors of vision are opened. It is because the different aspects of ecological life in natural areas are typically much safer than in tiny pockets of planted greenery in commercial gardens and parks. Oh, you'll get the normal sound of the water, the wind, the birdsong, and the rustling leaves. You can see the stars more plainly, too. In general, there is a different benefit for wilderness areas (what I refer to as woodland tang). Like I said, I believe that is mostly because the non-urban ecological environment is in great condition. Species variation is enhanced, biodiversity is increased, inter-species activity is increased, and thus human well-being is enhanced. Considering the environmental destruction currently being faced within the biosphere (and the fact that the biosphere can be used as a complex network with advanced organic technology), it was a no-brainer that this mindset needed to shift. Psilocybin has shown me that our assessment of life and evolution has been severely lacking and that longevity for our species depends on a correct understanding of what life on earth actually is. As a way of exploring the notion of natural intelligence in more detail than the allusions to it in previous pages, let me focus here on intelligence itself, in particular the notion of natural intelligence. For motives that I shall discuss shortly, let me bring to the table a rather shocking notion that alien intelligence has modified the human genome. Not a gentle intelligence or a passable intelligence, but a profound and strong alien intelligence, the kind of specialized intelligence you ought to stand back and gawp at. I'm bringing up this idea because such imaginary aliens would have the same kind of characteristics as we would have. In other words, we are alluding to the same kind of "strength" and acumen. The main difference is that the alien theory sees strong intelligence linked to deliberate beings, while the human intelligence concept sees knowledge and purpose linked to existence (ultimately to the rules and forces of nature).

However, according to the natural intelligence model, intelligence is fundamentally a mechanism rather than a substance, more like a verb than a noun. In fact, it is a mechanism involving the manipulating of information. We know that our brains process knowledge. This is achieved by nerve cells called nerves, firing and transmitting messages to each other. But it's easier to grasp that the biologic underpinning of the neuron is also a mechanism. However, all life — whether a person, a community of cells, a chimp's hand, or a portion of a chimp's brain that regulates hand movement — consists of processes requiring complex physical and chemical operations. What an astute biologic is the intellect

I'm always looking to. It's not that there's an essential spiritual power manipulating the biological strings, but rather that the biologic itself is an expression of knowledge, although unconscious. Life can thus be compared to a clever verb in practice.

One species of slime mold, called Physarum polycephalum, has recently been extensively studied by scientists. Physarum polycephalum is yellow and, while unicellular, can be seen with the naked eye and may have the look of a thin strip of slimy mustard. This is often present on decaying logs and can easily be confused for a yellow fungus. What the slime mold has done is to discover its immediate surroundings by sending tendrils to all areas of the labyrinth until it has found food. Once it has located the food, it removes all the "useless" tendrils and centers its body on the immediate path to the food. It was also found not to cover the ground that it had already visited, indicating that it could feel the slender tracks it had left before. The bottom line is that slime mold will solve the problem of how best to get food in a new and strange environment — even if it is unicellular and has no brain.

Unsurprisingly, perhaps, many scholars have heralded the slime mold in question as a type of rudimentary wisdom despite being devoid of gray matter. The term intellect is used to describe a particular kind of intentionally intellectual behavior. Since the maze-solving skills of the slime mold are considered intelligent, it is really not outside the pale to see all life as intelligent. Overall, if you think about it, the origin of life is strangely like the slime mold. As a result, life stretches out in all possible directions (through genetic variations) and those paths that tend to be beneficial (sensible habits that contribute to progress in the art of living and reproduction) are retained and improved, whereas "dead end" paths (genetic modifications that are harmful) are pruned away (i.e., "retracted"). That means that life is as big as a slime mold. And, to put it another way, the intellect of the slime mold is a recapitulation of the wisdom of the evolutionary cycle that has created slime molds.

It is important to bear in mind, though, that the intellect of a slime mold is extremely limited relative to life itself. Life has learned a lot more about how to get home from a meal supply. With regard to the question of sustenance, life has learned how to produce food (some of the animals plant mushroom gardens, for example), how to create food from photons of light (photosynthesis), how to capture food in a silk web (spiders), how to preserve food (think of nut-burning squirrels), how to graze food, how to eat food, and how to feed on apparently indigestible substrates (think of mushrooms and dung). Life is simply not a senseless and mindless thing, but instead an example of ever-adapting intellect, whether conscious or not.

The above case, in particular, focuses on the knowledge involved in the digestion process and on how to efficiently digest a potential food. How does a herbivore digest, say, grass (which herbivores feed on) that contains cellulose and is very tough? How does this redistribute the resulting high-energy molecules? Chewing alone is just going to divide the plant into smaller pieces. How do you practically reduce cellulose molecules to simplified components? It's an engineering problem, but one that life has overcome (by way of symbiotic bacteria, as it happens). And, like a slime mold exploring all potential solutions, life is a normal fluid wisdom that can still find a solution as long as a path exists and can be found by evolutionary means. Just be sure, we should extend the same kind of logic to this as to every other part of life that we care about. Printed loosely over the surface of the earth, life is a clever "protoplasmic film," forever morphing and communicating itself by various creatures whose art of living skills have been selected and strengthened by the greater structure of existence inside which this protoplasmic film is located. In short, nature is an intelligent system that provokes and sustains intelligent developmental mechanisms, mechanisms that create intelligent biologic systems. Therefore, intelligence is apparent on several occasions, from humans to creation, to the numerous natural laws and powers that control nature.

Unless the reader is already unsure about the use of the term knowledge, its core sense promotes more versatile use. The root sense is "choose from" (from the Latin inter legere). That is exactly what's going to happen for evolution. Of the many genetic possibilities that exist, the ones "chosen" and retained by the all-powerful hand of nature are those that make more sense, even as the slime mold tendrils that are "chosen" are the post-hoc sensible ones that come from fruit. It is the core of the experience of trial and error. It might not be a deliberate intellect, but it is still a certain type of intellect. While natural intelligence and natural knowledge are saturating the biosphere, we never seem to give them a second thought. To be sure, we think of the biosphere primarily as a collection of tools. What are we going to get from this forest? What are we going to remove and extrude from this ecosystem? What should we get out of this ocean? Why do we harness the chemical production potential of these bacteria? What crop genes can we combine to gain regulation of the global market? Why do we drain the lake or reshape the wilderness? The biosphere is so vast that our cavalier and blundering way of living has been unregulated for thousands of years. Now, though, our decimation of the world has hit a point of no return. Human activity is threatening the very dignity of the biosphere and exacerbating climate change. It has become practically difficult to go on trading as normal indefinitely. Everything needs to improve in the manner we respond to the rest of life on Earth. This is why I am asking for a new understanding on what life on Earth is.

CHAPTER TWO

History Of Magic Mushrooms

It is noteworthy that cultures unique to the American continent have encountered a comparatively high amount of natural mind-altering agents compared to early civilizations that developed in Europe or Asia. Botanical data does not support the idea that Europe has less hallucinogenic plants than other areas. In fact, the increasing number of newly discovered psilocybin-containing European mushroom species suggests that psychotropic mycoflora flourishes in Europe, close to what is found in other countries. Thus it is doubtful that early European cultures benefited less from the use and knowledge of native plants and mushrooms than cultures elsewhere in the world. More certainly, new indigenous knowledge of European psychoactive plants and mushrooms was lost or killed at some stage in history, possibly a few hundred years ago.

The discovery that the fly agaric mushroom (Amanita muscaria) was noted for its psychoactive properties in Siberia contributed to the conclusion that this fungus was probably used as a psychotropic agent in medieval Europe. In addition, there is very little documentation from the Middle Ages that suggests a universal understanding of the influence of particular mushrooms on human consciousness. However, I believe that previous studies on psychoactive mushrooms were causally related to Amanita muscaria precisely because, at the time, this was the only known psychotropic mushroom in Europe. While the use of Amanita muscaria by Siberian tribes has generated evidence of dramatic hallucinations, European accounts of agaric intoxication do not usually provide details of these highly hallucinatory effects.

As a result, the strong hallucinogenic properties of particular Psilocybes and similar organisms are likely to have had a much greater influence on early European populations than the delirium-like hallucinations caused by Amanita muscaria. This organism is often known to cause unconsciousness and serious somatic side effects. This theory is supported by evidence from extensive field studies undertaken in Mexico. I assume that historical records, including those mentioned below, suggest information and interaction with psychotropic mushrooms in Europe, most likely originated from the use of Psilocybes and similar plants, rather than from contact with Amanita muscaria. However, it is incredibly difficult to refute or affirm this theory due to the lack of conclusive evidence available for study today.

A Feast Of Fairies In Celebration Of The Spirit World

Tales of ritualistic mushroom use have made their way into the world of myths and legends. One legend, for example, mentions a rare poisonous fungus in Wales (British Isles) with the strange name of Bwyd Ellylon, which was considered a delicacy of the fairies that embraced the spirit world. Psilocybe semilanceata is the most common psilocybin-containing mushroom in Europe and thrives in areas of Great Britain, where the mushroom grows rapidly in the Welsh countryside throughout the autumn season. Several books chronicle countless witch-burnings in the area, with special focus on the witches' meetings at the Monte del Tonale, at an altitude of 2000 m (approx. 6,000 ft). Fieldwork has shown that plants of the nightshade family ('witching herbs') do not thrive at this altitude; only fly agaric mushrooms are rarely found there. On the other hand, the pastures in the region overflow with Psilocybe semilanceata throughout the fall. Considering this historical context, it seems possible that Psilocybe semilanceata played a significant role as a psychotropic agent in the field. In light of medieval accounts explaining the practice of witchcraft, it is important to remember that the subjective feeling of flight or levitation is one of the widely recorded symptoms of psilocybin intoxication.

Berserk Rage of Nordic Warriors

Many lines of wisdom have been destroyed in the wake of the religious power struggle between Christianity and the remains of the ancient sects that worshiped Nature. The systematic persecution and eradication of pre-Christian traditions have all but eroded the integrity of Europe's initial cultural history, along with a great deal of documentation recording early cultural activities, including the use of plants and mushrooms for the purpose of transient shifts of consciousness.

Several scholars have gone as far as blaming the fly agaric mushroom for the mythical "berserk fury" of the Viking warriors. Some sources describing this condition refer to the "deception of the brain" (i.e., auditory hallucinations). Since the custom of "going berserk" was outlawed by the Nordic legal system, it vanished quite abruptly during the 12th century. At around the same time, Saxo Grammaticus suggested that the Berserkers may have used magic potions. It is just as likely, though, to say that Psilocybe semilanceata, a species of mushroom very widespread in Norway, was the hallucinogen of preference for early Scandinavian cultures. Neither Amanita muscaria nor Psilocybe semilanceata are commonly considered to induce extreme rage. However, considering the historical context, it is likely that at that time people had already started to internalize unfairly distorted stereotypes and the demonization of psychoactive mushrooms and their effects was used in order to explain the development of new laws designed to eradicate repulsive pagan practices such as the ceremonial usage of mind-altering drugs.

It is important to remember the presence of ancient northern European stone drawings illustrating different themes of mushrooms, along with the discovery of bronze-aged vessels adorned with mushroom-related artwork. Drawings also contain depictions of zoomorphic beings as well as mushrooms. Significantly, both accounts and speculations about the Berserkers predate about 2,000 years. Such ancient illistrations demonstrate the emergence of early European mushroom cults- a spiritual tradition that most certainly disappeared during the early Iron Age, as did many other rituals and social traditions of that period. Still, the discovery of ancient Northern European mushroom cults is a strong piece of evidence supporting the idea that psychoactive consumption of mushrooms has been continuous throughout history.

Moreover, a traditional Swedish ritual has survived to the present day, disclosing the early knowledge of a certain mushroom claimed to invoke "visions of spiritual beings." A toxic mushroom fungus ('Baran') was tossed onto the bonfires as part of the summer solstice festivities. And though little is known about this fungus today, the annual burning of poisonous mushrooms was meant to disrupt the forces of goblins and other evil spirits. The mushrooms were used as abstract incarnations of noxious spirits. The ritualistic killing of the mushrooms by fire thereby suppressed the energies of nature and bad spirits. The belief that certain mushrooms have actual relations to the unseen forces of the spirit world may have originated from ancient scraps of evidence regarding the psychoactivity of different varieties of mushrooms.

There are a variety of published accounts of psychotropic mushrooms dating back to the late Middle Ages. Although this set of papers contains a number of various references from many continents, it offers strikingly consistent explanations of psychoactive mushrooms and the basic essence of their effects.

Love Potions Brewed From Boland Gomba

This fungus was known by the German name "Narrenschwamm" ("fool mushrooms"). It was used in rural areas, where wise men or "javas asszony" turned it into love potions. At around the same time, this "fool's mushroom" was also known in Slovakia. In addition, the mushroom found also refers to its capacity of "causing foolishness as opium does." Similarly, in England, John Parkinson's Theatricum Botanicum (1640) includes descriptions of a "foolish fungus." The Austrian colloquial phrase "He eats those mad-inducing mushrooms" applies to states of emotional distress.

Historical source materials such as these are rare. They definitely refer to psychotropic mushrooms but lack adequate details to allow for a consistent description of a particular species. However, considering the environments and occurrence of Psilocybe semilanceata and Psilocybe bohemica, these two species are among the possible candidates. It is interesting that these classic descriptions revolve around just one aspect of the ultimate effect of the mushrooms: the odd semi-schizophrenic reaction, which can also be quite dramatic. None of these accounts reflect a distinct reverence of the mushrooms like that of the Mexican Indian culture ("teonanacatl" = the flesh of the gods).

Between Reverence And Fear

By comparison, in Europe, signs of mushroom overdose have also been linked to symptoms of mental illness. These cross-cultural variations in value decisions can be explained in terms of two definitions introduced: mycophilia and mycophobia. This division subdivides societies with various typical mushroom views into two categories. For example, a deep-seated antipathy to mushrooms (mycophobia) in Britain suggests cultural attitudes that are radically different from those present in Slavic nations, where mushrooms are commonly revered (mycophilia). The origins and evolution behind these divergent views remain lost in the shadows behind memory.

The emergence of early cultural taboos and prohibitions against psychotropic mushrooms may be the root cause of long-lasting mycophobic behavior. On the other hand, it is likely that thousands of years ago, the practice of harvesting mushrooms as a food source triggered troubling clusters of regionally isolated cases of fatal mushroom poisoning. Such interactions might well have given birth to a strong and enduring aversion to the mycoflora of the world.

Similarly, the mycophilia characteristic of ancient Mexican cultures goes hand in hand with the general social approval of the effects of Psilocybe mushrooms and their known ceremonial uses. Among the Mexican Indian peoples, the symptoms of psilocybin have never been causally related to any known form of mental disorder. It is important to remember that the Indians of Mexico were the only Indians in the Americas who have cultivated a vast number of species of mushrooms for food. Unfortunately, our present socio-political climate is heavily skewed toward recently found hallucinogens, which are mostly characterized in terms of negatively charged logos. Worse still, this prejudicial reasoning distorts the rational, objectively impartial approach to the study of such drugs. The name "fool's mushroom" first appeared in the 1930s, along with "Mexican mushroom of madness." In the 1950s, Central American mushroom cults were discovered, and the mushrooms themselves were called "Mexican Magic Mushrooms" in honor of their psychotropic influence and to highlight the importance of early incorporation of the mushrooms into the social structure of the societies that revered them.

Earlier, the more benign name "hallucinogenic fungus" was used in mycological literature. Many designations that have gained and lost prominence over time include the rather derogatory word "intoxicating mushrooms" and the practically meaningless word "food mushrooms."

Scientifically Non-Biased Hallucinations?

Following his work with magic mushrooms in Mexico in the summer of 1960, a physicist returned to Harvard University and started researching psilocybin as a component through the usage of regular psychological research batteries. His original emphasis became blurred as he began to broaden his research to include increasingly wider environments and applications. In reaction to Leary's strikingly unorthodox approach, the American press started to describe psilocybin mushrooms in terms of slanderous language that far overshadowed the derogatory connotations of labeling, such as "fool mushrooms." Descriptions of the symptoms of mushrooms included reports that patients encountered "death-like conditions."

Proponents of psilocybin work are accused of arguing that the alkaloid produced "semi-permanent brain damage." This pseudo-scientific jumble of hollow jargon was symptomatic of the rapidly growing hysteria concerning hallucinogenic drugs. More and more news stories on psilocybin were replaced by news of LSD, advertised as the most potent hallucinogen ever found. The ensuing flurry of governmental efforts to regulate LSD resulted in ever-increasing limitations on scientific research not only of LSD but also of psilocybin. Mind-altering compounds were no longer spoken of in terms of their particular effects and properties but instead were put together into a single category of harmful chemicals. As anti-drug paranoia began to escalate, theoretical and pharmacological differences became all but irrelevant: hallucinogens were no longer viewed as separate from certain types of harmful and potentially addictive substances, such as cocaine or opioids. This demonization of hallucinogens was successful following major scientific attempts that started when Sandoz Pharmaceuticals agreed to administer psilocybin to trained scientists for diagnostic and psychotherapeutic purposes. Using the psilocybin synthesis system developed by A. Hofmann, Sandoz Pharmaceuticals developed approximately

2 kg (approx. 4.4 lbs) of pure psilocybin for medical research purposes.

The findings of pharmacological experiments quickly revealed psilocybin as an alkaloid that was completely healthy for human subjects under controlled laboratory conditions. Even given this data, the anti-drug regulatory paradigm of the mid-1960s strongly established "government mycophobia," an incorrect yet ingrained ideology that still prevails today and largely forbids the research of promising future applications for psilocybin and other alkaloids. Around the same time, mycological and biochemical experiments showed that psilocybin-containing mushrooms grow around the world and can be found on all continents. Such mushrooms are not distinct from all other mycoflora and must not be removed from the scientific study due to their alkaloid material.

In addition to the inherent variability of belief structures across societies, people continue to cultivate their own unique attitudes about mushrooms of general. Indeed, the evolution of common views on mushrooms can be traced back to childhood events, even though these early encounters seldom compensate for the emergence of dominant prejudices and belief structures later in life. I recall an incident that happened in my own youth when I was about five years old. I was playing in a grassy meadow when a girl pointed to a brown mushroom and explained that it was inedible and poisonous. Although I've never forgotten this experience, I grew up to become a committed mushroom enthusiast. On the other hand, another childhood occurrence left me with the vibrant recollection of seeing a wasteland nearly filled with a large number of gilled bluing mushrooms and the sense of wonder I've felt in considering this image. In fact, the peculiar features of these mushrooms are most likely responsible for the intense experiences of early childhood, which can then grow into specific behaviors or beliefs.

Persistent personal interest in psychotropic mushroom organisms, depending on the effect of other influences, may help to intensify or decrease mycophobic as well as mycophilic trends. Above all, decisions on the benefit or misfortune of deliberately modifying one's state of consciousness are often influenced by human desires, prejudices, and beliefs. Descriptions of anticipated and spontaneous studies with different types of mushrooms offer compelling proof that the effects of psychoactive mushrooms are subject to several potential interpretations.

The Popularity Of Psilocybe Semilanceata

Since the late 1970s, scientists in many countries have used state-of-the-art techniques (e.g. High-Intensity Liquid Chromatography) to check samples and measure their alkaloid content. More detailed analyses of these studies and their findings are given in the following pages.

Psilocybe semilanceata has specifically developed itself as a psychotropic genus of mushrooms in Europe. The species flourish in the continent of Europe, where significant work efforts have been made. In terms of use, Psilocybe semilanceata is the most common psychoactive species in Europe. Guzman's 1983 monograph indicates that Psilocybe semilanceata may well be the most common psychoactive Psilocybe mushroom in the world. While the species is known to grow in Europe, North America, Australia, and Asia, the mycoflores of other countries have not yet been identified or recorded. Therefore, we cannot yet determine the occurrence of Psilocybe semilanceata on a global scale.

The genus Psilocybe occurs most abundantly on moist pastures surrounded by woodland areas. From my experience, Psilocybe semilanceata grows in much of Germany's forests, fruiting in the period from late September to October. This species prefers acidic soil and grassy areas around the roads or along the edges of the trees. In general, species are organized into small groups of 30 mushrooms or fewer. Deer drops or other animal feces are usually found at these sites, even though the mushrooms rarely emerge directly on top of the dung. Occasionally, highly stunted specimens can be found in the mountains by the side of the road. The soil below the old cow pastures provides an excellent medium for extensive mycelial production. At certain places, large areas contain an excess of fruiting bodies, indicating the level of mycelial accumulation in the soil. Maximum yields can be anticipated given sufficient rainfall if the pasture has been grazed at least once in the weeks prior to the fruiting season. Most mushrooms also grow on horses and sheep pastures in varying conditions. These grassy areas within forests are typically breeding areas for deer, which offer extra fertilization to the soil. These pastures are often flanked by creeks or marshlands that saturate the soil with mud. However, Psilocybe semilanceata does not grow in areas where artificial fertilizer has been used.

During the summer, the warm climate in these wet areas provides an excellent environment for optimal mycelial development. In Germany, the mushroom habitat varies from coastal areas to mountainous regions, where specimens have been found at altitudes of up to 1,720 m (5,160 ft) above sea level. Samples were obtained in former Czechoslovakia at altitudes ranging from 330 to 1,000 m (1,000 to 3,000 ft) with a single site at 1,400 m (4,200 ft) above sea level. According to these patterns of distribution, the population does not seem to prefer a particular altitude. As of 1986, 44 sites had been logged in former Czechoslovakia, yielding a total of 54 samples. In comparison to other types of mushrooms, such as commercially produced white mushrooms (Agaricus bisporis), Psilocybe semilanceata can produce fruit at a much broader temperature range.

While Psilocybe semilanceata is widespread throughout Germany, it does not appear that the species prefers particular areas where it occurs in conspicuous abundance or density. One clear restriction on the growth of the plant is the use of fertilizer in areas that may otherwise be ideal places for mulch to flourish in. Very possibly, this is why the population has not spread to other environments in Germany in the past few decades. Descriptions of the extent of events in older literature are equivalent to recent findings.

On occasion, however, Psilocybe semilanceata can develop a significant number of fruiting bodies at some locations where the conditions for growth are excellent.

Between A Creek And A Marshlands Pond… 8½ Inches Tall!

At this point, I would like to provide some more information about the two marshlands where mycological fieldwork has been performed over a number of years. At the first site, the fruiting bodies formed in a shallow grass valley between very tall grass on mildly acidic soil. This grassy field became a woodland clearing between a stream and a marshland bog. Temperatures were slightly higher in areas exposed to direct sunshine than in the surrounding areas, a trend that continued through the fall season. Deer declines have led to the repeated fertilization of the field. The fruiting bodies of the first batch of mushrooms collected at this site had stems up to 8 1⁄2 in. [!] (21.5 cm) tall, due to the very high grass in the field. The mushroom caps were so small that it was not readily possible to specifically classify the genus as Psilocybe semilanceata. While a bluing reaction was present, chromatography testing was required to validate the organisms. Subsequent findings, though, resulted in species that could be classified on the spot on the basis of their morphological characteristics. At this site, we were able to collect 30 to 60 specimens every fall for three consecutive years. Shortly after, this lead to man-made improvements to the marshlands and the building of the access road.

Within the same year, we discovered a second position about half a mile from the first. The field was very wide, a former cow pasture that had been heavily grazed. It was situated close to a creek that absolutely filled the soil. Nowadays, sheep sometimes graze the field, and deer drops are usually found in hay. Here, in abundance, Psilocybe semilanceata fruits. The field is paved with hundreds of fruiting bodies per autumn season.

Over three years, we returned to the area three times per fall, collecting a total of 2,800 mushrooms (about 140 g or 5 oz. dry weight) at the field. Although some of the fruiting bodies could be readily spotted on grassy fields, the vast majority of the species were usually concealed within grass clumps. Psilocybe semilanceata is a readily identifiable genus when the air is warm. The fruiting bodies are highly hydrophanous, which is why the hue of the caps changes to a deep black-brown olive when the mushrooms are wet. Only a close examination of the gills and the crooked stems helped us to differentiate the wet mushrooms from the Panaeolus species. Like many other psychotropic mushroom fungi, the blue discoloration of the areas of the cap and the lower half of the stem is the main feature of Psilocybe semilanceata. While the degree of discoloration is comparatively high, it is especially visible when the mushrooms are damp. Fruiting bodies that are old and wet may randomly grow clear, blue stains around their caps. On the other side, the discoloration of the stems does not begin until the fruiting bodies have been removed from the mycelia for around 30 to 60 minutes. Even in areas with ample harvests, I have always encountered mushrooms with bluish-green discoloration among those that lacked this feature.

The blue coloring is retained during the drying process, although some fading can occur. The historical descriptions of the Psilocybe semilanceata described above are so detailed that I cannot add any better quality. Despite numerous views in the literature to the contrary, there is a strong scent coming from the moist fruiting bodies that have been opened up. This smell is similar but weaker than that associated with Psilocybe bohemica, which is sometimes described as suggestive of radishes or poppies but is usually not unpleasant.

In fact, mushrooms have a peculiar trait that never appears in other species. Under the light of a quartz lamp, the specimens of Psilocybe semilanceata transform fluorescent. In keeping with their intense psychoactivity, a high degree of psilocybin was found by chemical analyzes of Psilocybe semilanceata specimens. It is fair to assume that this strain has been more extensively researched than all other Psilocybe strains, including the Mexican version, the dried mass of which is estimated to contain 0.2-0.6 psilocybin. Psilocybe semilanceata specimens from Britain, Scotland, Norway, Denmark, Belgium, Holland, Germany, France, the United States as well as Switzerland and former Czechoslovakia were mainly studied. The combined study of multiple dried mushrooms for alkaloid content was found to have yielded an average value of 1% psilocybin per dry weight, regardless of country of origin.

The question of the chemical race has been fiercely discussed with respect to other species, such as fly agaric mushrooms. Nonetheless, unlike trees, such a mechanism has not yet been shown to occur in the higher species of mushrooms. To date, there is no evidence to support the notion that the basic chemical structure of a plant can differ significantly from sample to sample.

The Long Shelflife Of Psilocybin

Psilocybin is a relatively long-lasting compound as part of the dried mushroom tissue. A collection of desiccated mushrooms dated 1869 from the Finnish herbarium still contains 0.014 percent psilocybin. On the other hand, no alkaloids were detected in another study dated 1843. Sadly, it is no longer possible to establish the processes used to dry these samples. Temperatures above 50 ° C allow psilocybin to break down into its derivatives. In laboratory conditions, mushrooms are normally dried at room temperature. Fruits are occasionally freeze-dried for examination. Frozen mushrooms, however, have a highly porous texture that allows alkaloids to break down fairly easily if the samples are kept at room temperature (20 ° C). For this reason, samples frozen for biochemical analysis are processed at -10 ° C prior to alkaloid extraction or chromatography processing. In comparison to the findings from Finland, North American scientists have reported that psilocybin degradation is the slowest in Psilocybe semilanceata relative to other species.

In 1973, Semerdzieva and Nerud first documented the presence and qualitative value of psilocybin in the Psilocybe bohemica collections. This research team documented psilocybin levels of up to 1.1% in dried samples. The tests of my own research have shown variable amounts of alkaloids in various mushrooms obtained at one place near Sazava. Given the strong blue staining reaction, there is very little to no psilocin in the mushrooms of the European Psilocybe cyanescens family. European collections are somewhat distinct from Psilocybe cyanescens samples obtained in the Pacific Northwest of the United States by chemical-taxonomic criteria. It is considered to contain up to 1% psilocin (dried mushrooms) as well as a similarly high level of psilocybin (2% overall alkaloid content), making it one of the most active species in North America. The analysis of extracts taken from these mushrooms showed that ample psilocin was present for the oxidized compound to be detectable on a thin-layer chromatography plate. This was not the case when similar analyses were carried out on mushrooms obtained in former Czechoslovakia. However, mushrooms from both countries show similarly low amounts of baeocystin.

Generally, we can conclude that this highly psychoactive and visible animal is expanding its range across Europe. Improved use of nitrogen, soil acidification in many regions and the existence in every wet forest or park of a number of productive substrates, such as mulch, which is not dependent on the availability of dung, are all reasons that would possibly allow Psilocybe cyanescens to reach a relatively wide area of distribution in the future.

Growing On Dung, Manure, And Compost

The insanity tales, as well as the very name "dung-inhabiting" mushrooms, provide hints about the types of environments in which this species tends to grow. Often, they flourish directly on top of the dung or on the pastures that have been extensively fertilized. They are also present on garbage heaps, soil or straw substrates where mushrooms are commercially grown. European Panaeolus species that contain psilocybin have a special feature that separates them from Psilocybe species: very rarely do they grow blue stains when infected or wounded. In his description of the Scottish case of intoxication in 1977, Watling notes the conspicuous blue coloring of the stem caps of Panaeolus subbalteatus, which often formed in response to strain. The creation of blue stains is, according to my experience, very unusual. Statistics from the Pacific Northwest of the United States often claim that about one in a hundred mushrooms really turn blue.

One controversial topic in the literature is the toxicity of one species: Panaeolus foenisecii (Pers.: Fr.) Kuhn. This species has previously been known as Psilocybe as well as Psathyrella, and has been described as Panaeolina as opposed to Panaeolus, since it is a species that does not grow on dung, fruit only after hay harvest, and produces spores that are purplish-brown and abrasive. Many Panaeolus species, however, have black spore prints when mounted on white paper under a glass vessel to avoid dehydration. But also the spores of Panaeolus foenisecii (Pers.: Fr.) Kuhn may not always ripen at the same time, which can allow the gills to look mottled. Due to the complexities of taxonomic classification, there are no accurate maps showing distribution patterns for the European Panaeolus genus.

On May 25, 1986, in the village of Heringsdorf on the East German Sea Coast, at all stages of growth, I find 147 fruiting bodies of Panaeolus subbalteatus. They grew on a compost heap that originally included horse manure. By comparison to the Psilocybe species, Panaeolus mushrooms can be found at any point during the spring season. The distinction of the Panaeolus species is further hampered because they are very hygrophanous, with caps whose colors can range from white to blue, or from reddish-brown to very deep black-brown. Older mushrooms on the compost heap had caps that had broken with age, and edges that had curled outward and coated with spore particles. Just two mushrooms had blue-stained tops, and the stems did not change color in response to heat. Panaeolus subbalteatus has been called "Panaeolus variabilis" in American literature, as some of the stems mimic the appearance of certain types of mushrooms and thereby lead to taxonomic uncertainty. The fungus is also known to grow in the immediate vicinity of Panaeolus foenisecii (Pers.: Fr.) Kühn., providing more possibilities for error, particularly if the mushrooms are not closely inspected. The caps of Panaeolus subbalteatus grow flat as the mushrooms age, a characteristic that is taxonomically important.

The cape's long, watery marginal zone gives the mushroom its name. The psilocybin-producing organisms will be discussed in greater detail below. New detailed analyses show specifically that the Panaeolus subbalteatus is the most significant European psychoactive species in the Panaeolus genus. Ola'h's world monograph on the Panaeolus genus was written in the 1960s and created a great deal of controversy as he identified a variety of organisms as "latent psilocybin-producers." For example, he proposed that Panaeolus foenisecii sometimes release psilocybin. Both Panaeolus species share one trait that separates them from all other species: they produce 5-substituted indole compounds, such as serotonin and its biochemical counterpart, 5-hydroxytryptophan. Serotonin is a chemical commonly present in both animals and humans. It functions as a neurotransmitter in our brain, but not all of the actions of serotonin have been fully understood. However, it should be noted that both serotonin and 5-hydroxytryptophan are completely inert when ingested orally. When conducting paper or thin-layer chromatography, each of these compounds can easily be confused for psilocin. It is interesting that the reports of Ola'h contradict current studies, in that his research also revealed the presence of psilocin in Panaeolus animals!

The latest analyses of carefully selected mushroom material from the European Panaeolus genus have not reported large quantities of psilocin in these samples. Furthermore, "chemical races" identified with different species could not be created. I assume that nearly all unintended poisoning can be attributed to the consumption of Panaeolus subbalteatus, with the likely exception of one event caused by introduced tropical species. Too little is known in the literature on Panaeolus retirugis, its distribution, and chemical composition. Nevertheless, the addiction occurrence in Bremen suggests that this fungus is psychoactive. In 1985, I discovered two fruiting bodies in a field with a dry weight of 0.03-0.05 percent psilocybin, as well as serotonin. All the characteristics of the mushrooms, such as wrinkled, flesh-colored tops, corresponded to the accounts of the Panaeolus retirugis.

In addition to Psilocybe semilanceata, at least one other species of Psilocybe is known to occur in Europe. At this point, I will emphasize that the classification of single species within the Psilocybe genus is subject to considerable controversy among eminent taxonomists. For example, there are various methods of separating the Hypholoma gene from the Stropharia gene.

CHAPTER THREE

Essential Magic Mushroom Equipment

The legal status of acts concerning psilocybin mushrooms varies world-wide. Psilocybin and psilocin are classified in Schedule I of Medicines under the 1971 United Nations Convention on Psychotropic Substances. Schedule I drugs are classified as drugs with a high risk for abuse or drugs that do not have known therapeutic uses. However, psilocybin mushrooms have had many medical and religious applications in hundreds of cultures throughout history and have a considerably lower risk for misuse than most Schedule I drugs.

However, many nations have some level of regulation or prohibition of psilocybin mushrooms (for example, the US Psychotropic Medicines Act, the UK Abuse of Drugs Act 1971, and the Canadian Controlled Drugs and Substances Act). The legalization of psilocybin mushrooms has been opposed by the general public and academics who see therapeutic potential in relation to drug addiction and other mental instability, such as PTSD, anxiety, and depression. Among controlled medications, psilocybin mushrooms do pose fairly little medical risks.

There is some confusion about the legal status of psilocybin mushrooms in many national, state and regional drug laws, as well as a strong aspect of selective enforcement in some cases, as psilocybin and psilocin are considered illegal to possess as drugs without a prescription, but mushrooms themselves are not listed in these laws. The legal status of Psilocybe spores is even more ambiguous, as the spores contain neither psilocybin nor psilocin, and are therefore not illegal to be sold or possessed in many jurisdictions, although many jurisdictions will pursue, under broader laws, the prohibition of articles used in the manufacture of drugs. A few countries (including the United States of Georgia and Idaho) have specifically prohibited the selling and storage of psilocybin mushroom spores. Psilocybin mushroom cultivation is known to be a drug development in most jurisdictions and is often harshly penalized, although some countries and one US state have ruled that cultivating psilocybin mushrooms do not qualify as a controlled substance.

Psilocybe azurescens is a psychedelic mushroom genus whose major active compounds are psilocybin and psilocin. It is one of the most active tryptamine-bearing mushrooms, releasing up to 1.8 percent psilocybin, 0.5 percent psilocin, and 0.4 percent baeocystin by dry weight, with an average of around 1.1 percent psilocybin and 0.15 percent psilocin. It belongs to the Hymenogastraceae family in the Agaricales class.

Pileas: The cap (pileus) of Psilocybe azurescens is 30–100 mm in diameter, conical to convex, deeply convex and gradually flattening with a pronounced, constant, thick umbo; smooth base, viscous when wet, protected by a separable gelatinous pellicle; brown to ochreous to caramel in color, sometimes pitted with dark blue or bluish-black patches, hygrophanous.

Gills: the lamellae are descending, sinuate to adnate, dark, and sometimes stained in black when injured, near, with two layers of lamellae, often mottled, with white margins.

Spore Print: Spore print is deep purplish-brown to purplish-black in density

Stipe: 90–200 mm in length and 3–6 mm in width, silk-white, dingy-brown at base or age, hollow at maturity, and consisting of bent, cartilaginous tissue. The base of the stem thickens downwards, is frequently bent, and is distinguished by flat white aerial tufts of mycelium, often with azure tones. The mycelium covering the stem base is deeply rhizomorphic (i.e., root-like), silky smooth, keeping the wood chips together tenaciously.

Taste: highly salty

Odor: odorless to fragrant.

P. azurescens occurs naturally in a small section of the U.S. West Coast, including the regions of Oregon and California. It was also found as far south as Depoe Bay, California, and as far north as Grays Harbor County, Washington. The key locations are clustered around the delta of the Columbia River: the first picks were made in Hammond, Oregon, and Astoria. It's also very common in Oregon, North of the Columbia River, from Long Beach South to Westport. Some wild collections have also been reported in Stuttgart, Germany. Frequently, mushrooms can sometimes be grouped near deadwood in the Oregon Valley of Willamette. Ilwaco, Washington still has a huge population, but mining is a potential felony if discovered by local law enforcement officials.

The natural habitat of the species ranges from caespitose (growing in low, separate clusters) to gregarious deciduous wood chips and/or sandy soils rich in lignicolous (woody) debris. The fungus is related to the grass of the coastal dunes. It produces a broad, dense, tenacious mycelial mat (collyboid) in appearance. P. azurescens helps whiten the wood. Fruiting begins at the end of September and continues until "late December and early January," according to mycologist Paul Stamets. Psilocybe azurescens has been cultivated in many countries, including Germany, the Netherlands, New Zealand, the United Kingdom, and the United States (especially California, New Mexico, Ohio, Oregon, Vermont, Wisconsin, and Pennsylvania).

Step By Step Guide Process Of Growing Magic Mushrooms

More and more people are cultivating psilocybin mushrooms at home. As well as having secure, year-round resources, domestic cultivation reduces the possibility of misidentifying wild mushrooms. It's also a fun, low-cost hobby for many growers. If you don't know how to grow the mushrooms in your home, you could be tempted to start with a psilocybin mushroom growing kit. Such ready-to-use packets provide a live mycelium substrate (the substance behind the growth of the mushroom) that, technically, you only need to keep moist.

In reality, you are better off starting from scratch. Having your own layer is not only more durable but if you do it properly, it will also be less susceptible to pollution. There isn't a big price gap, though, so you'll end up knowing a lot more.

Background

The PF Tek system revolutionized the indoor growing of mushrooms. The main breakthrough was the application of vermiculite to a grain-based substrate (as opposed to the use of grain alone), allowing mycelium more room to expand and imitating natural conditions. While this approach is a little more labor-intensive than others and despite its potential for lower yields, its flexibility, low cost, and efficiency make it suitable for beginners. It also uses easily available products and ingredients, much of which you might already have.

Spore Syringes

The one thing you might have trouble getting is a proper spore syringe. It will hold the magic seeds of mushrooms, which will be used to "sow" them onto the soil. Some growers reported pollution concerns, misidentified varieties, and even syringes containing nothing but water. However, as long as you carry out your homework and find a reliable source, you're not going to have any issues.

In any case, after you have grown your first batch (or flush) of mushrooms, you can start filling your own syringes.

What Variety Should I Choose?

When you know how to cultivate mushrooms indoors, you're going to want to settle on a genus and strain. Many vendors have a variety to choose from, but Psilocybe cubensis B+ and Golden Teacher mushrooms are among the most common for beginners. Though not as strong as some others, such as Penis Envy, they are stated to be more tolerant of sub-optimal and changeable conditions.

Ingredients and Equipment

Spore syringe, 10-12 cc

Organic brown rice flour

Vermiculite, medium/fine

Drinking water

Equipment

12 Shoulderless half-pint jars with lids (e.g., Ball or Kerr jelly or canning jars), Drill with a ¼-inch drill bit, Hammer and small nail, Small towel (or approx. 10 paper towels), Mixing bowl, Strainer, Heavy duty tin foil, Measuring cup, Large cooking pot with a tight lid for steaming, Micropore tape, Clear plastic storage box, 50-115L, Perlite, and a mist spray bottle.

Hygiene Supplies

Air sanitizer, Rubbing alcohol, Surface disinfectant, Butane/propane torch lighter, Sterilized latex gloves (optional), Surgical mask (optional), and Still air or glove box (optional)

Instructions

The simple PF Tek approach is very straightforward: Prepare your brown rice flour, vermiculite, and water substrate and split it into sterile glass jars. Introduce spores and wait before mycelium grows. This is a network of filaments that will support the growth of your mushroom. Move your colonized substrates or "cakes" to a fruiting chamber after 4-5 weeks and wait for your mushrooms to develop.

NOTE: Please maintain proper sanitation before starting: spray air sanitizer, properly wash your appliances and surfaces, take a shower, brush your teeth, wear clean clothing, etc. You don't need much space, but your room should be as sterile as possible. Opportunistic bacteria and molds can proliferate under many conditions, so it is crucial to mitigate the risk.

STEP 1: PREPARATION

1) Clean the jars:

- Place the nail and hammer (which can be cleaned with alcohol to disinfect) four holes in each of the lids, precisely spaced across their circumferences.

2) Prepare substrate:

In a mixing tub, add 2/3 cup vermiculite and 1/4 cup water with each glass. Drain the remaining water with the disinfected strainer.

Apply 1/4 cup of brown rice flour per half-pint container to the bowl and mix with wet vermiculite.

3) Fill bottles:

- Be careful not to stack too closely, fill the bottles in half an inch of the rims.
- Sterilize this top half-inch with rubbing alcohol
- Fill up the bottles with a waterproof vermiculite coating to insulate the ground from the pollutants.

4) Heat sterilize:

- Tightly screw the lids and coat the bottles with tin foil. Protect the edges of the foil along the sides of the bottles to prevent water and condensation from escaping into the openings.

- Put a small towel (or paper towels) in a large cooking pot and put the jars on top to ensure that they do not touch the surface.

- Bring tap water to the point halfway up the sides of the jars and bring to a steady boil, ensuring that the jars stay upright.

- Put the tight-fitting lid on the pot and steam for 75-90 minutes. When the pot is running dry, refill with hot tap water.

NOTE: Many farmers use a pressure cooker set at 15 PSI for 60 minutes.

- Upon steaming, leave the foil-covered jars in the container for several hours or overnight. For the next move, they need to be at room temperature.

STEP 2: INOCULATION

1) Sanitize and clean the syringe:

- Use a flame to heat the length of the needle of the syringe until the red syringe is dry. Enable it to cool down and clean with alcohol, taking care not to touch it with your mouth.

- Push the plunger a little and rotate the syringe to disperse the magic spores of the fungus equally.

NOTE: When the spore syringe and needle need to be installed before use, be exceedingly careful to prevent contamination in the process. Sterilized rubber gloves and a surgical mask can assist, but the best option is to place the syringe inside a disinfected still air or a glove box.

2) Inject spores:

- Cut the foil from the first of the jars and push the syringe as deep as it reaches into one of the openings.
- About 1/4 cc of the spore solution (or marginally less by using a ten cc syringe over 12 jars) is applied with the needle touching the surface of the jar.
- Repeat for the remaining three holes, rubbing the needle with alcohol between the holes.
- Close the gaps with the micropore tape and set the bottle aside, leaving the foil out.
- Continue the inoculation cycle with the remaining bottles, sterilize the needle with the flame, and then the alcohol between the tubes.

STEP 3: COLONIZATION

1) Wait for mycelium:

- Store your inoculated jars clean and out of the way. Prevent direct sunshine and temperatures south of 70-80 ° F (room temperature).

- Pale, fluffy-looking mycelium will begin to emerge between 7 and 14 days and spread out from inoculation sites.

NOTE: Watch for any signs of pollution, including unusual colors and sounds, and dispose of all suspicious bottles immediately. Do so outside in a safe pocket without taking off the lids. If you are uncertain if the bottle is infected, always lean to the side of caution — even if the soil is otherwise well colonized — because certain chemicals are lethal to humans.

2) Consolidate:

- After three or four weeks, if all goes well, you will have at least six well-colonized bottles. Enable the mycelium to reinforce its grip on the substrate for another seven days.

STEP 4: PREPARING THE GROW CHAMBER

1) Make a shotgun fruiting chamber:

- Take your plastic storage container, drill ¼-inch holes approximately two inches apart around the bottom, base, and top. To stop from splitting, hammer the holes in a piece of wood from the inside out.

- Set the box over four solid items, positioned at the corners to allow air to pass below. You may want to cover the surface beneath the package to shield it from moisture leakage.

NOTE: The shotgun fruiting chamber is far from the ideal concept, but it's simple and easy to create and does a decent job for beginners. You will want to seek alternatives later.

2) Remove perlite:

- Put the perlite in a strainer and run under a cold tap to drain.

- Allow it to drain till there are no drops remaining, then scatter it over the base of your growing chamber.

- Repeat between 4-5 inches deep with a perlite base.

STEP 5: FRUITING

1) "Birth" of the colonized substrates (or "cakes"):

- Open your jars and separate the dry vermiculite coating from each one, taking care not to disturb your substrates or "cakes" in the process.

- Empty each container and tap onto the disinfected surface to release the cakes intact.

- Clean the cakes one at a time under a cold tap to avoid any loose vermiculite, again taking care not to hurt them.

- Fill your cooking pot or another large container with tepid water and put your cakes inside. Submerge them with another pot or equivalent heavy object just below the top.

- Keep the bowl at room temperature for up to 24 hours to rehydrate the dish.

- Clear the cakes from the water and place them on a disinfected sheet.

- Cover the mixing bowl with solid vermiculite.

- Roll the cakes one by one to fully cover them with vermiculite. That is going to help hold in the moisture.

- Cut the tin foil square for each of the cookies, big enough for them to rest on without touching the perlite.

- Place these equally spaced within the rising container.

- Place the cakes on top and softly foam the spray bottle in the container.

- Cover fan until closing.

- Put the chamber four times a day to keep the temperature up, taking caution not to soak the cakes with water.

- Open fan up to six times a day, particularly after misting, to improve airflow.

NOTE: Some farmers use 12-hour fluorescent lighting, but indirect or ambient lighting during the day is perfect. Mycelium requires only a little light to decide where the open air is and where the mushrooms are to be positioned.

STEP 6: HARVESTING

1.) Watch for fruits:

- The mushrooms or fruits will start as tiny white bumps until they sprout into 'balls.' After 5-12 days, they will be able to harvest.

2.) Choose your fruit:

- Chop the mushrooms near to the cake when about to be added. Don't wait for them to hit the end of their development, as they tend to lose control as they mature.

NOTE: The safest time to pick the mushrooms is before the veil breaks. At this point, they're going to have small, conical-shaped caps and protected gills.

STORAGE

Psilocybin mushrooms tend to go bad in the refrigerator after a few weeks. And if you're going to use them for microdosing, or simply want to store them later, you'll need to think about storage. Drying is the most efficient approach for long-term storage. This will keep them healthy for two to three years as long as they are kept in a calm, quiet, dry spot. When they're put in the fridge, they're going to last forever.

The lo-fi way to dry your mushrooms is by leaving them on a sheet of paper for a few days, maybe in front of a fan. The drawback of this approach is that they're not going to be "cracker tight." That is, they're not going to break as you want and stretch, which ensures they're always going to hold any moisture. These can also decline dramatically in effectiveness, depending on how long you keep them out. Using a dehydrator is a more effective process, but it can be costly. A suitable option is to use the desiccant as follows:

Air-dry the mushrooms for 48 hours, preferably with a fan.

Place the desiccant coating at the base of the airtight bag. Ready-to-use treats include silica gel kitty litter and anhydrous calcium chloride, which can be bought from hardware stores.

Put a wire rack or similar set-up over the desiccant to prevent the mushrooms from touching it.

Place the mushrooms on the rack and make sure they are not too crowded together and seal the jar.

Wait a few days, then check to see if the cracker is intact.

Transfer to plastic bags (e.g., ZipLoc, packed vacuum) and put in the freezer.

Reusing The Substrate

After the first flush, you can re-use the same cakes up to three times. Simply dry them out for a couple of days and repeat Stage 5.2 (Dunking). But don't attempt to roll them in the vermiculite; just bring them back in the rising chamber and the fog and the fan as before. When you begin to see the chemicals (usually after the third re-use), dip the mister spray cakes and dispose of them outside in a clean container.

Making Spore Syringes

Filling your own psilocybin spore syringes is as self-sufficient as it gets. You'll need to take a spore print from a mature mushroom, that is, one that's allowed to expand until the cap is removed and the sides are twisted up. You will also note an aggregation of dark purple particles around the foundation. These are the magic spores of the mushroom.

To gather them, cut the cap with a flame-sterilized scalpel and place it on a clean sheet of paper. Cover with disinfected glass or bottle to shield from the air and set for 24 hours. Hold the resultant spore printed out of the sun in an airtight plastic container.

To fill a spore syringe, scrape some of the spores in a clean container of purified water. You can find this in a car parts shops. Then fill the syringe (which must also be sterile) and pour it back into the bottle several times to disperse the spores equally. Fill it for the last time and place it inside the airtight plastic container. Leave at room temperature for a couple of days to allow the spores to hydrate. You should keep the syringe in the refrigerator until you're able to use it. It should last at least two months.

Adaptations And Alternatives

Numerous improvements have been made to the PF Tek process, both to maximize yield and to make it simpler. Specific organisms also tend to perform best under specific substrates and environments.

The key solution to the simple PF Tek is the monotub process, which involves bulking on coir (coconut fiber extract), manure, straw, or some other fresh and nutritious substrate. Ultimately, you may want to play with any of these other approaches, but for now, PF Tek is a decent introduction.

How long does it take to cultivate magic mushrooms in your home?

The time it takes for the mycelium-colonized substrate to grow harvestable fruits depends on a variety of factors. But the entire cycle of growing mushrooms will take about 1-2 months.

How are you going to pick shrooms?

You will be able to harvest the fruit 5-12 days after it starts to sprout from the mushroom substrate.

The key is to extract them before the veil falls, i.e., until they mature and unleash their spores. In other words, the gills are yet to be developed. Your mushrooms should also have small, conical caps at this point.

How can I render a spore syringe?

We also included instructions on how to create a spore syringe above. You may need a sterilized knife or scalpel, a clean paper towel, and a disinfected glass or container to extract psilocybin spores from a mushroom that is allowed to mature. Add the spores of the fungus to a container of clear water and apply the sterile syringe. After keeping it at room temperature for a few days to hydrate, it can be kept in the refrigerator for at least a few months.

How do you cultivate mushrooms at home without spores?

Use the Psilocybe cubensis grow package if you don't want to add the spores of the mushroom yourself. The standard cubensis growing package comes with an already colonized substrate for growing mushrooms in a pack. They are suitable for various types of cubensis, as well as for different animals. Even the magic mushroom growing kits aren't without their detractors.

What's wrong with using a magic mushroom growing kit?

Despite their apparent simplicity, magic mushroom growing kits are commonly seen as a waste of time. And if they work at about the same price as beginning from scratch, their contents and consistency are unknown. They could also be more susceptible to pollution. Using app comments, they cannot really function. At best, they show contradictory outcomes. If nothing else, using a cubensis grow kit isn't going to show you how to grow magic mushrooms from scratch.

What's the right mushroom substrate for you?

While tried and tried by generations of mushroom farmers, brown rice flour and vermiculite substrate may not be the right option for all. It depends on your expectations. Brown rice flour is perfect for bulk growing, but coir could be cheaper and simpler to use. Then there's whole brown rice (not flour), which is expected to yield more powerful berries.

Pasteurized horse manure is another viable choice as it is rich in phosphate, nitrogen, and potassium. And tossing spent coffee grounds into the mix (up to a quarter of the total) could help speed up colonization. Of note, the expended coffee grounds are also economical; 99 percent of the coffee biomass that does not end up in the cup is typically just thrown away.

Some growers claim that the right mushroom substrate is full of nutritional diversity. Too many nutrients from several sources can, however, contribute to pollution. For a beginner, it's best to keep it simple – not to mention inexpensive enough for trial and error.

What's the difference between magic mushroom spawning and substrate?

When you know more about cultivating mushrooms indoors, you are likely to see the words 'spawn' and 'substrate' used almost interchangeably (or even incorrectly).

Clearly placed, the 'substrate' (brown rice flour / vermiculite cakes in the PF Tek method) will become 'spawn' if it is used to colonize a second 'bulk substrate' (coir, manure, etc.) in the fruiting chamber.

When you are fruiting directly from the cakes as instructed by this document, the mushroom substrate retains the 'substrate' even after it has been separated from the bottles.

What are the safest varieties of Psilocybe cubensis?

As shown in the guide, some of the most common P. cubensis strains (or varieties) for beginners are B+ and Golden Teacher mushrooms. Experienced growers would prefer Penis Envy. However, as with the choice of your substrate, the best cubensis strain for you would depend on your preferences for the cultivation of mushrooms.

How do you produce magic truffles?

Forget about the idea of growing mushrooms in a box; truffles are mostly grown in jars instead of in a fruiting chamber. For info, see this Tek. Another main distinction to PF Tek, as described above, is the use of a boiled rye (aka rye berries) base. Common varieties of truffles include P. Mexicana and P. tampanensis, also known as 'philosopher stones.'

Where can I find supplies to grow mushrooms?

One of the big things about the PF Tek system is that supplies are readily available. What you don't already have sitting around the house can be found in the nearest hardware store. The only thing you need from a professional manufacturer is the first shipment of psilocybin spores. The easiest way to locate a credible one is through a forum.

CHAPTER FOUR

Effects Of Magic Mushrooms

Psilocybin mushrooms can be eaten in their whole form. They're normally fried, and most people accept that they don't taste good. The alternate approach is to make psilocybin mushroom tea. Some people prefer to place the mushrooms in peanut butter or Nutella to disguise their flavor.

What to anticipate: A normal trip with a mild dose of psilocybin mushrooms (1-2.5 g) provides an elevated severity of emotional stimuli, heightened introspection, and impaired neurological processing in the form of "hypnagogic stimuli "— a transitory period between sleep and wakefulness. Brain MRI experiments indicate that a psilocybin ride is neurologically similar to a dream flight.

Perceptual changes, such as visions, synesthesia, mental swings, and a blurred perception of time, are all typical of a psilocybin journey. Such effects are typically experienced an hour or two after an oral dose.

You will begin to note improvements in your visual perceptions, such as light and object halos and geometric shapes, even while your eyes are closed. Your feelings and perceptions will begin to shift. It's not uncommon to have a sense of vulnerability to emotions and feelings that you prefer to ignore in your daily life. A feeling of joy and pleasure in the world around you, the people in your life, and your feelings are also very normal, along with a sense of calm and a sense of harmony with the universe.

You can have intense feelings, both positive and negative. Seek not to fight these thoughts, but let them run their course. Many who report strong negative emotions often report a parallel sense of relaxed recognition and separation, particularly if they remind themselves that emotions are transient.

Physical side effects can differ from person to person, including changes in heart rate (up or down), changes in blood pressure (up or down), nausea, decreased tendon reflexes, tremors, dilated pupils, restlessness or agitation, and issues with synchronized activity.

One study has shown that psilocybin can induce headaches that can last up to a day in some individuals. However, none of the participants reported serious headaches, and psilocybin is currently used to treat a psychiatric disorder called cluster headaches (see the section on medicinal uses).

Phases of a Psychedelic Mushroom Trip

The four main phases of a Mushroom Trip are intake, initiation, trip (peak), and downfall. Each step comes with its own collection of experiences and observations, with peaks — usually a few hours after ingestion — resulting in the most extreme sensory and psychological changes. No matter the process, it's important to relax and realize that what you're feeling is temporary, and there's nothing to stress about.

Bad Trip

Someone who is eager to try psilocybin mushrooms for the first time might be afraid of having a "bad ride" at any stage. Dysphoric visions, uncontrollable anxiety, and imprudent actions are among the more popular worries. Bad trips are common, but risks can be reduced by adhering to the psychedelic experience of the 6S. Being well trained and mindful of the reasons before experiencing an LSD experience will help mitigate the risks.

Interactions with Other Drugs

Coffee: a funny reality! It may be a match made in the interstellar stratosphere. Not only are there no known adverse side effects of combining the two, there is also a coffee maker in Denver that does so deliberately.

Marijuana: no known dangers, but it also has the ability to intensify the addictive quality of the mushrooms.

Adderall, Xanax, Zoloft: all are effective psychoactive medications whose side effects are entirely arbitrary. Psychedelic use should be treated with great caution when using these drugs daily.

Potential Benefits

Psychedelic mushrooms have a long-standing, deep, and well-established history in the many cultures that have traditionally used them. Nowadays, the advantages of these strong little fungi are commonly known. Research on the common and multi-faceted use of psychoactive mushrooms is widely ongoing in the United States and overseas. One such study published in the Journal of Psychopharmacology showed that "a single dose of psilocybin induced significant and permanent reductions in depressed mood and anxiety, along with an increase in quality of life [...]." In fact, the mysterious and transformative experiences that so many people encountered since psilocybin entered the American psychedelic lexicon in the 1960s are only starting to be examined and investigated in traditional medical research. The findings are convincing and persuasive and present a well-founded, optimistic, symbiotic image of mushrooms as an effective healer.

Specifically, research trials have been ongoing in the United States and overseas, targeting people with life-threatening cancer. The key purpose of this research is to clarify the effectiveness of high-dose psilocybin delivered in medical settings as a method to relieve psychiatric pain and distress frequently associated with a life-threatening diagnosis. The findings have been positive so far. Under double-blind settings, even just a single, high dose of psilocybin has been found to alleviate symptoms of psychiatric distress in terminal patient groups; the results have been significant and lasting.

In addition, there is a growing body of evidence that indicates that part of why psilocybin is so powerful is that it causes neuroplasticity. That is the capacity of the brain to learn and develop and evolve.

In early studies in which psychedelics were administered to healthy adults under favorable circumstances, multiple participants reported long-term positive improvements in their temperament, behavior, beliefs, and attitudes. Anecdotal accounts have also corroborated these initial observations as people frequently show greater love of music, art and nature, increased empathy towards others, and a heightening ofcreativity and imagination after a psilocybin mushroom ride.

Such early observations have also been mirrored in more recent research. Approximately 40% of participants in laboratory studies of psilocybin reported significant, long-term improvements in visual perception and their relationship to nature.

Analysis in 2011 showed that more than a year after a single encounter with psilocybin mushrooms, the accessibility of identities remained substantially elevated in the study subjects. Scientists are speculating that the magical aspect of a mushroom ride is likely to be the secret to any positive improvement.

We describe the mystical experience as "feelings of harmony and interconnectedness among all persons and objects, a sense of sanctity, feelings of peace and happiness, a sense of transcending natural time and space, ineffability, and an unconscious conviction that perception is a source of empirical truth regarding the nature of life."

Such subjective effects — such as sensations of interconnectedness — of psilocybin mushrooms are possibly due to their tendency to increase the interconnectivity of brain communication hubs. That is, psilocybin makes more "cross-talk" between brain regions that are normally kept apart. Researchers believe that this allows a state of "unrestricted awareness." Many of the same forms of brain activation are often found in specific stages of meditation.

Recent work has shown that psilocybin can be used to strengthen spiritual activity. The broad research enrolled 75 participants who participated in a six-month spiritual course involving meditation, mindfulness, and self-reflection. Throughout the study, participants received either a small or a high dose of psilocybin. At the end of the six months, patients with a high dose of psilocybin reported substantially stronger changes in indicators of spirituality such as emotional closeness, sense of life, a transcendence of death, and redemption.

Therapeutic Use

Several preclinical studies in the 1960s and 1970s indicated a potential role for psilocybin and other psychedelics in the treatment of cluster headaches, mood disturbances, and addiction. Since the federal government reclassified psilocybin as a Schedule I drug in the 1970s, research into its clinical efficacy has been practically non-existent until recently. The anecdotal accounts of the medicinal benefits of psilocybin have now caught the attention of scientific practitioners and regulators.

Psilocybin in the Treatment of Cluster Headaches

Intense but shorter in duration than migraines, cluster headaches are often described as the most severe and debilitating form of headache. Attacks at night can be more traumatic than those that occur during the day, but they also have a huge effect on a person's life.

To date, no rigorous trials have been conducted documenting the ability of psilocybin to combat cluster headaches, although a number of observational findings have captured the attention of the scientific community. In the mid-2000s, medical practitioners started considering psilocybin and LSD as alternative therapies for cluster headaches after some of their patients reported remission of their disease after experimental psychedelic use (and eventual self-medication).

A new study found that psilocybin could be a more effective cure for cluster headaches than commercially approved treatments, with almost 50 percent of patients citing psilocybin as a totally effective treatment.

Psilocybin in Depression and Anxiety Disorders Therapy

Anecdotal reports pointed to psilocybin (and other psychedelics) as a cure for depression disturbances such as depression and anxiety. Psychologist and psychedelic expert Dr. James Fadiman has been gathering anecdotes for a number of years, the vast majority of which are optimistic.

The federal government has approved several limited, highly regulated trials to be performed on the therapeutic potential of psilocybin for mood disorders. A pilot was performed in 2011 to test the effects of psilocybin on stress and end-of-life anxiety in terminal cancer patients. Patients in this study had advanced cancer and a psychiatric history of depression or anxiety due to their illness. Researchers observed major changes in stress and anxiety interventions up to six months following psilocybin therapy. This research was subsequently awarded the status of Phase II by the FDA.

Previously, a prominent medical group in London published a report claiming that psilocybin could be used to combat severe depression. Twelve patients received two doses of psilocybin (one low and one high) along with therapeutic help. One week after the second dose, depression levels were greatly decreased in nearly all cases, with eight of the 12 cases displaying no signs of depression. Three months on, five patients were still free from depression, and four of the other seven had a decrease in their depressive level from "Severe" to "Mild or Moderate." Psilocybin treatment has also been found to significantly alleviate symptoms of obsessive-compulsive disorder (OCD) in a clinical group of patients who did not respond to traditional serotonin reuptake inhibitors (SRI). During this study, participants reported a reduction of OCD symptoms ranging from 23 percent to 100 percent.

Psilocybin in the Treatment of Addiction

"Classic psychedelics" have been used in preclinical experiments to cure depression in the 1950s and 1960s with positive outcomes, but once again, all of these psychedelics have been deemed illegal. In the U.S. and most of Europe, research into using them in a medical sense has come to a complete halt. Nevertheless, recent years have seen a revival in the use of psilocybin and other psychedelics as medical devices for the treatment of addiction.

In a 2015 study, psilocybin was found to be effective in the treatment of depression as part of an aided recovery program. Significant decreases in alcohol and abstinence were reported following the administration of psilocybin as part of the recovery plan.

Psilocybin is also a possible method to help people avoid smoking cigarettes. In a new report, two to three therapy sessions of psilocybin as part of a broader cognitive-behavioral smoking cessation care plan had an 80 percent smoking cessation progress rate among the test participants (12 out of 15 subjects). In contrast, traditional smoking quitting success rates — using gum, patches, cold turkey, etc .— have about a 35 percent success rate.

Is Psilocybin Re-wiring the Brain?

Some experts are starting to suggest that much of the positive effects of psilocybin on mental health problems could be due to its capacity to "reset" the control system in the brain. The Default Mode Network (DMN) was associated with depression and other mood disturbances when overactive. Psilocybin has been shown to significantly decrease the activity of DMN and has recently been linked with its anti-depressant effects.

LSD vs. Psilocybin

LSD and psilocybin mushrooms (also called psilocybin) are perhaps the two most widely used psychedelics. Most people, though, ask about the disparity between them.

Common questions include:

How do you know about LSD and psilocybin mushrooms?

Do psilocybin mushrooms feel more "normal" than the LSD?

Are there different kinds of visuals?

Are psilocybin mushrooms "safer" than LSD (or vice versa)?

Why use LSD vs. psilocybin mushrooms?

Is there a disparity between cocaine and LSD?

While LSD was popularized by mass usage in the 1960s, psilocybin mushrooms have been used in shamanic rituals for centuries. Like other psychedelics, psilocybin mushrooms and LSD have commonalities in how they affect human consciousness. Popular effects include hallucinations, thoughts of isolation or dissatisfaction, and ego removal. Yet, as someone who eats both LSD and psilocybin mushrooms will tell you, there are also major variations.

LSD Facts

Psychoactive in micrograms (millionths of a gram)

LSD is the simplified term for the chemical compound lysergic acid diethylamide. It is often referred to as "acid," and doses are often referred to as tabs that define the tabs of blotter paper on which the LSD can be added

Synthesized in 1938 and first used in the early 1940s

Derived from ergot, a fungus that usually grows on rye

The average dosage is between 100 and 250 microg.

Psilocybin Mushroom Facts

Used after 1000 BC

The average dosage of psilocybin is about 10-40 mg – which amounts to about 1-4 g of dried mushroom

Dozens of various varieties of mushrooms containing psilocybin

The trip lasts from 6-8 hours

No risk for physical dependency

Available for legal purchasing in the form of psilocybin truffles

Decriminalized in several areas in the U.S.

'What will I experience when taking LSD vs. psilocybin mushrooms?'

While each personal experience varies, anecdotal accounts suggest similar phenomena.

The following reports can help you prepare for your own experience. Keep in mind that these results arose from the use of a small dosages (LSD: 100-250 micrograms – psilocybin mushrooms: 2-4 grams). Microdosing of these compounds (about 1/10th of a normal dose) can yield different outcomes.

Psilocybin Mushrooms vs. LSD Effects

What are the Effects of LSD?

While using it is better to communicate with sober people, if possible. This leads to a more "extro-spective" approach.

An LSD trip is more likely to stay optimistic. Fills consumers with bubbly, optimistic feelings.

Consumers describe their LSD experience as better and with less body load than psilocybin mushrooms.

Very prone to configuration and design. Through monitoring these two factors, you are much more likely to get a successful ride.

What are the effects of Psilocybin Mushrooms?

These contribute to the ego-drop and full harmony of the self and cosmos.

Most people feel more related to nature and the environment by using psilocybin mushrooms.

Constantly on the move between a positive and a bad trip – feelings are more unpredictable and contradictory.

"Come up" can be more painful

Users show more introspective interaction, totally losing contact with sober truth.

How to take LSD vs. How to take psilocybin mushrooms

LSD typically comes as a pill, or as a book, gel, or candy that has the LSD dumped on it. Paper tabs are the most common and are left to disappear under the tongue. Psilocybin mushrooms are generally simply consumed in their dried state, or often ground into powder and stored in capsules or added to food or drink.

The biggest difference between the two is the flavor. Pure LSD should be tasteless, and psilocybin mushrooms have a rather unusual earthy taste. Both LSD and psilocybin mushrooms can induce queasiness, but this can also be due to an empty stomach or jittery nerves.

LSD vs. Psilocybin: How long does it take to kick in? How long is it going to last?

Apart from the longer-lasting effects of LSD (up to 12 hours compared to 6-8 hours on mushrooms), the time of initiation and development of both drugs are also different. It's not too obvious at first, but LSD appears to kick in a bit faster - only 30-45 minutes- compared to psilocybin mushrooms, which usually take about an hour.

For mushrooms, you appear to "max" around 80 minutes after ingestion, whilst LSD may take a few hours to reach the feeling of peaking. The LSD journey is also long enough to produce several peaks, whereas psilocybin mushrooms normally last only long enough for one important peaking moment.

LSD vs. psilocybin mushrooms: Visual effects

Psilocybin mushrooms are more likely to create visual effects than LSD. Hallucinations are uncommon when LSD is used. For LSD, it is more common to view objects or structures as throbbing or "breathing" and see the leftover signs of moving objects. LSD has visual effects that are similar to cognitive effects, and objects appear sharp and tidy, while colors appear more vivid despite being real.

Psilocybin mushrooms have more sensory effects, where static objects move or turn, and even entire entities or items may appear. Color can be highly influenced, and the colors of everything will combine into a cohesive scheme or pattern — for example, the entire universe may appear to be seen through a purple or sepia prism.

LSD vs. psilocybin mushrooms: Emotional and physical symptoms

The neurological symptoms of LSD and psilocybin mushrooms are very distinct. LSD certainly shifts and affects perception, but still, it retains a paradoxical sense of knowledge even in the midst of uncertainty.

With psilocybin mushrooms, you are far more likely to feel out of balance and remove yourself from your sense of self and normal life. This can be soothing, but it can also be disorienting and intense.

Physically, LSD appears to generate crisp, slightly nervous energy. Often you need to switch around quickly to better control it, or it can turn into fear or restlessness. Psilocybin mushrooms tend to have more rooted physical effects. You feel strong, deeply rooted, and, particularly while outdoors, deeply connected to nature. Both drugs also have beneficial effects on the relationship between the mind and the body.

Below are a few quotations from the internet that accurately explain the distinctions between LSD and psilocybin mushrooms:

"With acid, you feel like you're driving a motorcycle, with psilocybin mushrooms, you feel like you're in the back seat for a trip."

"Acid feels like you're tapping into the world while shrooms you feel like an ancient tree wandering in the trees."

"Mushrooms are for planting, LSD is for spreading your roots."

"Psilocybin mushrooms are sensitive to me. In many ways, they are a completely different ballpark. Mushrooms lack the consistency, the 'perfectness' of LSD, yet they provide a certain attribute that sometimes contributes to deep introspection ... 'Golden Teacher' has not won its reputation by mistake.

LSD is more elegant ... it helps me feel more emotionally aware, with more exposure and understanding into my own feelings. 'Golden Teacher' is more fine-grained ... it always makes me look, powerful and anywhere ... the images are liquor. They're taking you along."

(On the" body high "of psilocybin mushrooms) "It's a pretty big difference because LSD doesn't have a lot of body travel, at least not a comparable one ... LSD is a lot more cerebral."

"Shrooms feel a lot more 'druggy' to me. I always get a buzz that's like LSD with a little touch of trippity mixed in."

What About Both?

There is definitely a chance of consuming LSD and psilocybin mushrooms together. Nonetheless, that may be a challenge. Both drugs are often overpowering, and the consumer lacks comprehension and control. A proper dosage of both substances is important.

If you are considering trying LSD and mushrooms together, it is strongly recommended that you first get familiar with each drug separately. A successful beginning strategy will be to minimize the dosage of each particular drug by about a third and to be prepared for an unpleasant experience.

There are a number of positive stories from taking LSD and psilocybin mushrooms together, where the peculiar visual effects and loopy mood of the mushrooms are improved by the sharpness and purity of the LSD. But mixing the two compounds is effectively another matter worth a separate review. The big question remains:

Which Psychedelic Should You Try?

Many claim that LSD is harder to handle at the beginning. But it also lends itself to a more pleasant atmosphere, and a lot of people find insightful and outgoing energies more fun. Psilocybin mushrooms, on the flip side, may be preferable to those wanting an extreme, grounded, and visually stimulating experience. It's "earthlier" and more rooted in many respects, so it can drive you away from your "self." It can be daunting, which isn't always a bad thing. Regardless of the unpredictable and daunting aspect of psychedelics, it's best to try to make your first encounter a pleasant one. Whether you're looking to try LSD or psilocybin mushrooms for the first time, be sure to do your homework and dive in.

Why Microdose With Psilocybin Mushrooms?

When you have a healthy way of thinking and don't have convenient access to an organic chemistry lab to synthesize LSD, microdosing of psilocybin mushrooms is a safe choice to explore. Although snipping or diluting blotter tabs is a simple way to microdose with LSD, it entails a reliance on an external source that might not be accurate or effective. Purchasing legal psilocybin truffles, or even better, cultivating your own psilocybin mushrooms, leaves you in control of the operation, and if you have a golden-brown thumb, you may find yourself supplying microdose-enthusiast buddies with your mushrooms.

Microdosing with psilocybin mushrooms is perfect for hands-on psychonauts who enjoy the thought of being involved in every step of the process. Preparing psilocybin for microdosing requires a little investment in kitchen supplies, but you can quickly find everything you need for about $80.

So You've Got Some Psilocybin... Now What?

If fresh psilocybin mushrooms are what you have at hand, especially if they are tiny miniature pinheads that have never matured, it can be enticing to think along the lines of "Microshrooms for Microdosing." There's something instinctively organically appealing about the idea of just taking a little mushroom cap in the morning along with your coffee and cereal. However, this would most likely result in an inaccurate psilocybin microdosing experience. Have respect for the following:

Wet and dried psilocybin mushrooms are usually considered equal with a dried to a wet ratio of 10%. Know, though, that this is just an estimate, and fresh mushrooms can be more or less than 10% of their dry weight. It means that if you take 3 grams of fresh mushrooms, you will take more or less than 0.3 grams of dried mushrooms, based on the mushroom itself and environmental conditions, such as humidity levels.

The caps and stems contain psilocybine. The psilocybin content of Psilocybe cubensis, one of the most widely produced varieties, is 0.37–1.30 percent in the entire mushroom, with 0.44–1.35 percent in the cap and 0.05–1.27 percent in the base. This implies that the caps are, on average, marginally more potent than the roots, and there are tiny parts of roots that have virtually no psilocybin. In order to equalize, it is often advised to grind the mushrooms intpo a fine powder.

Psilocybin content differs from mushroom to mushroom, from flush to flush, and from strain to strain. Changing variations during the microdosing regimen will make calibration challenging because you will be ingesting different quantities of psychoactive material for each form of psilocybin mushroom.

The composition of psilocybin varies at various stages of the mushroom growth. Miniature pinheads that didn't really grow bigger can be more effective than larger mushrooms per gram of weight.

If you take a microdose of psilocybin truffles, you should be mindful that dried truffles also have less psilocybin than dried mushrooms – see the weighing and measuring section on the various amounts you can use.

Under-microdosing yourself is much less of a concern than unintended over-microdosing. Finding yourself talking to the ceiling while you try to cross things off your to-do list is not only unproductive; it will raise your level of anxiety.

Storing Magic Mushrooms

Fresh mushrooms and truffles can be kept in the refrigerator at 2-4 degrees Celsius for up to a month. They should be sealed in a cloth bag or wrapped in an unbleached kitchen towel. The cold and dark conditions of the refrigerator are ideal for storing them, but the moisture in the refrigerator will inevitably affect the growth and decomposition of bacteria. This is particularly true for mushrooms. Truffles, due to their lower moisture content, can also comfortably last three months if vacuum-sealed in a ziplock container. However, in order to preserve psilocybin mushrooms longer, they must first be thoroughly dried.

Drying mushrooms removes moisture and stops bacteria from developing. This can be achieved in a variety of different ways. Methods range from placing them on a blanket, leaving them in front of a fan, to heating at low temepratures in the oven for a few hours (this is a mistake, as any heat will decrease their potency), or keeping them in a bowl of Epsom salts.

The complete, thorough drying process often requires the initial step of pre-drying, where the mushrooms are put out in the sun under a dark cover, or in front of a fan, for a few hours until their texture becomes gummy, and their appearance becomes wrinkled. After that, a desiccant has to be added. It can be either a personalized Epsom salt-based concoction or a plain box of silica gels. That way, the drying of the mushrooms is gradual; it takes a few weeks for them to enter the crackling state typical of complete dryness.

However, for convenience, energy, and time savings, a low-heat food dehydrator is one of the most efficient ways to preserve psilocybin mushrooms while keeping their potency level intact. A dehydrator can set you back just under $40, and when you don't need it to make cracker-dry portals to a different dimension, it can makes banana chips as a decoy. Several mushroom harvests can be dried overnight in a dehydrator instead of leaving them on all the surfaces of your house for weeks. Dehydrators are especially recommended for humid climates.

If completely cured, all mushrooms and truffles can be kept in a cold, dry location for a few years or longer (if you don't lose or consume them in this time frame). The loss of potency will be limited or non-existent if there is no sun, humidity, or heat to interfere with the psilocybin inside.

How To Prepare Psilocybin Mushrooms For Microdosing

Grinding the dried psilocybin mushrooms into powder is by far the easiest way to create the most effective psilocybin microdose. Through grinding the mushrooms together, you homogenize the psilocybin content difference between caps and stems, both from the mushroom to the seed.

The best way to pulverize psilocybin mushrooms is with a curry or coffee grinder. Unlike the dehydrator, it is advised to provide a different one for the processing of microdoses, because it is extremely difficult to extract all the small mushroom particles from the blades. Although it may be fun to picture your roommate unwittingly enhancing herself when grinding spices for chai tea, it is better not to run the risk of unintended microdosing.

Practical Tip: It will require less than a minute to pulse the psilocybin mushrooms into a fine powder. Do not open the grinder for at least half an hour to allow the fine dust to settle. Opening it right away would allow the disturbed spores to be drawn into the air and anoint your kitchen with the scent of magic fungi for hours. Note that weed is not the only thing that can cause the feeling of inhaling atmospheric vapors.

Weighing And Measuring: How Much Makes A Psilocybin Microdose?

Using an electronic kitchen scale is a good place to start. Scales correct to 0.1 – 1.0 grams are around $20. Weigh the dry mushrooms out before the process of pulverizing to see how much gross mushroom mass there will be once they are pulverized. Understanding how many you need to proceed with will help you split the doses for each microdose.

For example, 2 grams of dried whole mushrooms yield ten microdoses of 0.2 grams after powdering.

You need about one-tenth of a normal dose to microdose mushrooms. It means that you may need between 0.2 – 0.5 grams of dried psilocybin mushrooms per dosage. (If you are utilizing psilocybin truffles, use between 0.5 – 1 gram of dried powdered truffles per dose – they should contain less psilocybin than mushrooms).

However, note that this dose can be higher or lower based on the neurophysiology, weight, and potency of the mushrooms or truffles that you are microdosing and will depend on the user. A significant aspect of the microdosing process is calibrating the dose to make it a good match just for you. This cycle may take a few microdoses to sort out, so it's best to start low and then (patiently) build-up before you hit a sweet spot for your psilocybin.

Generally speaking, if a usual microdose is 0.2-0.5 grams of mushrooms, you'll want to start with 0.1 grams if your body weight is below 100 lbs. However, if you weigh around 200 lbs, you would be fine starting at 0.3 grams. Double the initial doses for truffles.

Kitchen measurements are also not precise to 0.1 grams. You will not detect any weight until at least 0.5 grams are available, and that may be too much for a single microdose. In this case, just dump all the material onto a sheet of paper and sort it equally into micro-piles.

As you may note, the trouble with powdered mushrooms is that their low density allows the powder to float everywhere while handling. And, as I stated before, try not to breathe too much of the air, or you're going to give yourself aerial microdoses. When you don't want to go through the hassle of manually separating the material, there are other methods to disperse microdoses:

Mushroom capsules: Mushroom tablets, or capsules filled with an identical dosage of mushroom powder, are the perfect choice because of their accuracy. This requires a capsule filling dispenser. These contraptions, which cost around $240, will charge several capsules at the same time by distributing the powder uniformly around the capsule holder. This is a common approach for the dedicated micro (or macro) doser, and it has the advantage of bypassing the loamy mushroom flavor that not everyone loves. The downside is that the quantity that fills the capsules is pre-determined so that the doses are pre-assessed, and it's easier to change the dose after the mushroom tablets have been prepared. Therefore, you can only use this approach once you have defined the optimal dose. When that is finished, you should blend the mushroom powder with something like cocoa powder or powdered sugar in the amount required to fill the capsule to hold the optimal amount of psilocybin.

Mini scoops: Just place all the mushroom powder in a little jar and use a very little scoop (1/16 to 1/8 of a teaspoon) to weigh the doses. The benefit of this strategy is that you can change your dose more flexibly on the go, and you can do it even though you don't have a scale. The downside is that it is less precise.

Combination: Use small scoops to weigh and fill the psilocybin microdose into the capsules. This is a way to microdose mushrooms with no taste and gives the versatility to adjust the dosage per request.

Consuming A Psilocybin Microdose

If you've calculated the volume of your microdose, there are other ways to absorb it. We've already been over the possibility of a mushroom pill; another commonly used option is to make a mushroom drink, or you can try to be innovative and blend your mushroom or truffle powder with something you ingest in your daily life.

Mushroom tea is simple to make and softens the flavor, particularly if you add honey. It's made much like every other tea. Just pour hot water over the mushroom powder and stir until the mixture is homogeneous. You could also apply the microdose to your wellness shake in the morning, or mix it with the maple syrup that you put on your pancake breakfast, or infuse it into the chocolate icing that goes on top of your brownies. You can even just add it to your coffee or tea, but the substance is insoluble in liquids, so it remains in little clumps in your cup. Sprinkling over cereal is one way to hide the earthy flavor, as is adding it to orange juice or a spoonful of honey. A lot of people just like the substance as it is. There are infinite possibilities.

The Importance Of Intention For Microdosing Mushrooms

Be mindful of your microdose motives when you take your dose. Microdosing provides the best effects because you're still aware enough inside yourself to know that you're doing it.

What Types Of Magic Mushrooms And Truffles Can Be Used For Microdosing?

You may use any kind; people most commonly opt for classical strains such as Golden Instructor (Psilocybe cubensis) or Liberty Caps (Psilocybe semilanceata). Since the small dose causes a subperceptual effect, there should be no clear variation in the strain used. If you note any results, you've taken too much; consider dialing back before you hit your sweet spot.

How To Grind Magic Mushrooms Without Using A Grinder

While no other method would be as precise (and accuracy is crucial to microdosing), you can go the old-fashioned way of using scissors to pulverize them as finely as possible. For this scenario, a highly sensitive digital scale would be important, because eyeballing it would add a second degree of imprecision to the dose amount.

What If I Take Too Much Or Too Little?

When you take too little, you're not going to feel a thing. When you take too much, depending on the pressure, you can experience some drowsiness or other emotional hyperactivity. The trick is to locate the dosage just below the point where you see the effect.

Is Microdosing Mushrooms Safe?

Taking appropriate (meaning, not incredibly high) doses of psilocybin have been shown to be absolutely safe. Of course, taking a microdose is also safe. However, there hasn't been a systematic study on repeated microdosing over a longer period of time, so we encourage users to take a microdose for no more than a couple months at a time.

Can A Psilocybin Microdose Be Detected In A Drug Test?

Psilocybin and its metabolites are not screened for in any of the mainstream drug tests. However, they can be detected in expanded medication scans.

CHAPTER FIVE

Common Problems In Growing Magic Mushrooms

Growing magic mushrooms takes skill and a working knowledge of some basic principals. Identifying these growing challenges and learning how to handle and avoid them will help you become a wise and effective magic mushroom grower. Here are some of the top challenges which can arise even for the most expert grower.

Spore syringe issues:

One of the most common problems faced during the early stages of raising mushrooms is the use of a spore syringe. As discussed in previous chapters, a spore syringe is a spore tube used by farmers to disperse spores to the soil. Contamination, misidentified strains, and vendors supplying water-only syringes are the most common issues consumers have.

The only way to prevent this dilemma is to use a trustworthy supplier. You will be able to find a good manufacturer using the recommendations of other magic mushroom producers, reputable web outlets, and people who have grown a specific form of magic mushroom you want to plant. When you've successfully grown your first batch of magic mushrooms, continue by filling your own syringes and storing them so you don't have to buy any more.

Contamination of mushroom crops (pollution of bacteria and mold):

Seed contamination can be caused by bacteria or mold. If your crop is completely invaded by bacteria or mold, your mushrooms will be made worthless. If you don't move fast, a tiny speck of mold could turn into a web of destruction and waste all your time and energy. Here are a few tips to keep your growing environment clean.

Before you start growing your mushrooms, clean your growing region thoroughly. Use surface disinfectants, bleach, and sanitizers to scrub the materials and appliances which come into contact with your crop.

Have a butane or propane torch burner to use on your devices. Torching or heating tip tweezers and other useful equipment is a simple but easy way to sterilize them. You should also have extra butane or propane cans ready to refill your torch lighter when needed.

You can use an air sanitizer to clear the air of damp and harmful odors. Air sanitizer is different from air freshener as it actually improves the smell of the atmosphere without eliminating any harmful microorganisms.

You must also have bins of clean gloves and surgical masks in order to avoid contamination from your skin. Many molds and bacteria are transmitted by contact, and these protective devices can help prevent the dissemination of microorganisms. It's also important to take a shower, brush your teeth, and put on clean clothes.

If you see a strong bacterial or mold infection in your crops, address it immediately. Eliminate infected tubes, culture disks, and other polluted devices from the environment. Wash and sanitize your containers with surface disinfectant and sanitizing machines before you start growing a new crop.

Pest control

A variety of pests can wreak havoc on your mushroom harvest, and the only way to avoid it is to be careful. One such recurrent type of pest is the gnat of the fungus. This is a winged beetle that is very attracted to mushrooms. It feeds on the body of the mushroom by tunneling and swallowing the mushroom tissues. It will take only a few hours for an infestation to happen, and then all your hard work will be in vain.

There are a few ways to handle the infestation of gnats. Thoroughly clean the area where your mushrooms grow. Remove any garbage or waste in the vicinity of the building. Sanitize the environment well. Prevention is always the best cure.

Harvesting problems

Growing mushrooms can be a challenge, and you may end up spoiling your mushroom crop and failing if you don't know when to pick your mushrooms. The fruits may start as white bumps before they grow stems and in just five to twelve days, they'll be set for harvest.

To harvest them, cut the mushrooms close to the cake and remove them. Don't wait too long or, as they mature and hit the end of their growing season, they will lose their potency.

Storage problems

Another typical issue is the using the correct method of storage. Psilocybin mushrooms will go bad after just a few weeks in the refrigerator. If you want to use a batch that you have developed for microdosing, you need to think about where to store it. Drying is the most effective way to preserve the mushrooms for a long time. Drying magic mushrooms can preserve them for two to three years. That is as long as the dried shrooms are stored in a cold, dry, dark spot. If the dried mushrooms are stored inside the fridge, you will be able to preserve them for an infinite amount of time. (Methods of drying are discussed in previous pages)

Problems with deciding on a mushroom species and strain

Many species of mushroom are suitable for first-time growers or newcomers, although others are only for seasoned growers. Learning about the various varieties of mushrooms and the different growth conditions of each one should allow you to take care of your crops and avoid any problems.

The best species for inexperienced growers include Psilocybe cubensis, B+ and Golden Teacher varieties. These are tolerant strains and can thrive even in sub-optimal growing environments and conditions. Do your homework before you determine which species you want to develop.

What Possible Pollutants Can Arise In The Mushroom Crop?

Most specialty mushrooms are cultivated on sterilized substrates, and if a contaminant has a foothold, it can survive in the absence of competition from other pollutants. Throughout nature, intricate relationships with hundreds of different fungi, bacteria, nematodes, etc. create an ecological equilibrium. Within a sterilized atmosphere, the grower offers optimal conditions for the contaminant to survive.

Wet Spot, Sour Rot - Bacillus sp

Within grain spawn bottles, one usually finds Bacillus, which often survives the sterilization cycle as heat-resistant endospores. It may appear as a dark-gray to mucus-like brownish slime characterized by a foul odor that is variously described as smelling like rotting apples, dirty socks, or burnt bacon. Bacillus makes the uncolonized grain appear wet, thus the name "Wet Spot." This contaminant is distinguished by pallid to white ridges along the margins of individual grain kernels. Bacillus reproduces mainly by simple division of cells. In times of adverse environmental conditions, particularly heat, a single hardened spore develops bacterial endospores within each parent cell body that can withstand high temperatures for a prolonged period of time.

The most practical approach for removing bacterial endospores requires soaking the grain at room temperature 12-24 hours before sterilization. Endospores, if active, should germinate within the time-frame and become vulnerable to normal sterilization procedures. Thus, in this damp setting, new endospores do not enter the remaining grain container.

Bacterial Blotch-Pseudomonas tolaasii (P. fluorescens)

This appears as yellow to brown lesions on mushrooms. Usually, spotting occurs on or below the edge of the mushroom caps. Blotch happens when mushrooms stay damp for 4 to 6 hours or longer after the water has been added. The bacterium is transmitted by airborne soil particles. Controls include reducing humidity and watering with 150 ppm chlorine solution (use calcium hypochlorite products because sodium hypochlorite products can burn caps). Nonetheless, if the mushroom remains moist, chlorine has no effect as the bacterial population reproduces at a rate that neutralizes the influence of the oxidizing agent. Shiitake caps are infected by bacterial diseases caused by Pseudomonas gladioli (Burkholderia gladioli). The sanitation process is a vital component of control initiatives.

Cobweb mold or Dactylium Mildew- Hypomyces sp.)

A cottony mycelium grows on a covering. Once it gets into contact with a fungus, mycelium quickly envelops the fungus with light mildew of mycelium, which induces a strong rot. It's also a wild mushroom parasite.

Cobweb mold is thicker than mycelium and is almost brown relative to white. The contrast of color is also hard to distinguish for someone who hasn't seen them side by side before. Cobweb has a variety of other traits, one that stands out being the pace of production. A little spot the size of a penny will expand to cover the whole jar/casing in just a day or two. Cobweb also has very delicate threads, while mycelium appears to be longer strands.

Cobweb mold is favored by high moisture content. Control techniques include reducing humidity and/or increasing movement of air.

Yellow Mould-Harzianum, T. Viride, T, man. Coningii Green Mold

This mold is formed by Trichoderma harzianum and is distinguished by an offensive, white mycelium that develops over the casing and on the mushrooms causing a soft decay. The mass of spores that ultimately develop is emerald green. Strong infested manure fields are barren. It is actually the most significant crop illness in United States agriculture. Most farms add salt to the soil in the contaminated areas when green mold is first found.

Good sanitation is essential. Shelving, trays, walls, doors, etc. can be surface disinfected as a part of course, but this must be done with a sense of urgency following the spread of the disease. Many commercial products are available for surface cleaning. The basic ingredients in these materials include chlorine, iodine, phenol, or quaternary ammonium, among others. Surface disinfectants are used on a farm-wide basis, from sanitary equipment to room washing downs to foot-dip solutions to pre-wash basket harvesting. Other green molds can be better defined as indicators because they do not seem to be as aggressive as T. Harzianum, man. These Trichoderma species also sporulate on the surface of the casing and may sporulate on infected mushrooms. These fungi indicate that carbohydrates are available, possibly due to insufficient nitrogen supplementation during Phase I or under composting. T. Viride is reported to produce toxins that dissolve the walls of the mushroom cells. Wet compost low in ammonia before pasteurization, bees, poor hygiene, anaerobosis, and other influences can allow green mold. These fungi are abundant in sawdust and are used in the processing of specialty mushrooms.

Trichoderma is often mistaken for Aspergillus molds (and vice versa), as both look very similar and are impossible to tell apart without the use of a microscope.

Cinnamon Brown Mold-Chromelosporium fulva (Peziza ostrachoderma)

The color of this mold varies from yellow gold and golden brown to cinnamon brown. It grows quickly in circular patches. It is very prevalent in natural soil and thrives on moist trees. Areas of compost overheated during spawning can be colonized. Improperly treated compost can also sustain growth but is most widely recognized as a re-colonizer of excessively pasteurized casings, likely surviving on dead microorganisms. It also happens on sterilized soils. Sexual fruiting bodies can appear a few weeks after the first appearance of the mold. Spores are in the soil.

Lipstick Mold-Sporendonema purpurescens (Geotrichum candidium)

This fungus colonizes soil or casings. When the spores mature, the color of the mold varies from white to purple, to cherry red, and eventually to dark brown. Spores scatter in the soil, in the watering process, and on pickers. The lipstick mold uses other fats in the compost. It's a very rare issue. Proper methods of sanitation should control it.

Pink Mold, Red Bread Mold-Neurospora

This is commonly seen on agar and feed. Neurospora replicates exponentially, often taking just 24 hours to fully colonize a media-filled Petri dish. It is widespread in nature, found in dung, soils, and dead plant matter. Because this fungus spreads through cotton stoppers or filter disks, a single infected container, though sealed, may disperse spores to neighboring spawn jars inside the laboratory. It is most commonly caused by the filter disks or cotton plugs being even the least bit damp; or if the ambient humidity is high. In fact, Neurospora spores germinate more quickly at high temperatures. The pink mold found in mushroom production is most widely known as Neurospora sitophila, a pernicious contaminant that is difficult to remove. Any infected crops should be removed from the laboratory as early as possible and burned. It is extremely important to disinfect the laboratory thoroughly. If damage continues, remove all the spawn and continue anew.

Sepedonium Yellow Mould-Sepedonium spp.

This thin, coarse mold grows in the compost throughout the spawning cycle. It turns dull yellow to brown with age. The thick-walled spores are in the soil and can withstand high heat. The mold colonizes compost as it is ideal for spawning production.

Black Whisker Mold, Doratomyces spp.

This fungus produces black powdery spores, which, when disturbed, appear as smoke. This mold shows the existence of other nutrients in the soil during the spawning season. The proportion of carbohydrates, especially cellulose, may be too high. Black whisker mold is also found in compost that has been overheated during spawning. Easy carbohydrates are used by this fungus, but lignin can also be used. Doratomyces, Aspergillus, and Penicillium contain a significant number of spores that may cause respiratory symptoms (nasal that throat inflammation, lung congestion, trouble breathing, etc.).

Blue-green molds-Penicillium spp.

Abundant blue-green spores are formed at the surface of the substrate. It's similar to Aspergillus. The ideal conditions are similar to those of the black whisker mold. These use basic carbohydrates as well as cellulose, sugar, fat, and lignin. These fungi are very widespread in specialty mushrooms and are one of the major concerns in agar and grain cultivation. Spores are both diffuse and pervasive.

Black Mold (including Yellow Mold and others)- Aspergillus sp.

These are quite popular in the cultivation of agar and grain, and in the processing of compost. Located on most organic substrates, Aspergillus favors near neutral or mildly simple pH. Well-used wooden trays and compost shelves are popular sites for this contaminant. Species range in color from yellow to green to black. Aspergillus species are most often greenish and similar to Penicillium.

Aspergillus niger, as its name suggests, is black; Aspergillus flavus is yellow; Aspergillus clavatus is blue-green; Aspergillus fumigatus is grayish green, and Aspergillus veriscolor has a number of shades (greenish to pinkish to yellowish). Like several others, these molds change color and texture according to the medium in which they exist.

Any form of Aspergillus is poisonous. Aspergillus flavus, a yellow to yellowish-green plant, produces toxic aflatoxins. A.

Flavus targets cottonseed crops, peanuts, and other oil-rich seeds that have been processed in dry, moist conditions. Among all the biologically developed poisons, aflatoxins are the most active hepatocarcinogens ever detected. The toxicity of this strain was largely unknown until, in 1960, 100,000 turkeys were suddenly destroyed by an epidemic of this disease in the United Kingdom.

A. Flavus grows on nearly all forms of food, a subset of which is of significant concern to the mushroom spawning farmers. Careful attention to the detection of all molds, in particular those of the Aspergillus genus, should be the primary responsibility of a mushroom farmer.

Aspergillus niger and Aspergillus fumigatus, two thermotolerant mesophiles, are both localized pathogenic to humans. They cause a disease called aspergilliosis or "Mushroom Worker's Lung Disease." Spent compost is the most natural source of Aspergillus fumigatus.

Oedocephalum (Brown) Mold-Oedocephalum spp.

This mold develops a light gray growth on the compost surface, which then turns brown as the spores mature. It forms an erect spore-bearing structure with spherical clusters of large spores at the top end. Its ecology is close to that of Coprinus and also occurs with Coprinus.

Olive Green Mold-Chaetomium spp.

The fruiting structures of this mold look like an olive-green cauliflower-1/16 inch in diameter-which grow on the compost. While its heat-tolerant spores live for 6 hours at 140 F, the mold occurs only in compost inappropriately handled during Phase II, particularly where phase II ventilation is insufficient. Lack of oxygen when compost temperatures are higher than 142 F permits the formation of compounds formed under anaerobic conditions. Both chemicals are harmful to the production of the offspring, but they are used for the olive green mold. It's very cellulolytic.

Pin Mold - Rhizopus spp.

This is a very fast growing fungus. When sporulated, it forms several large aerial hyphae decorated with black-headed cones. It grows on easily available carbohydrates. Together with Aspergillus and Penicillium, the members of this genus are the primary pathogens in grain spawning. It's very common on straw, too.

Thielavia thermophila,Trichothecium spp., Plaster Molds, and Flour Molds-Papulaspora byssina, Botryotrichum piluiliferum, and others Such molds grow when phase I nitrogen supplies (ammonic compounds and amines) are not fully utilized by the microbes during phase II and when the nitrogen is not converted to microbial protein. They're often seen in untreated compost. Aerial hyphae accumulate on the top of the soil, resembling plaster of Paris. White plaster (Botryotrichum piluiliferum) forms thick white colonies. T. Thermophila is thermophilic (unique among indicator molds) and may grow rapidly during the last days of Phase II. It indicates hot spots during spawning, inhibiting spawn growth (resulting in black areas). Brown plaster mold (Papulaspora byssina) forms dense brown colonies of compost.

Mummy Disease - Pseudomonas aeruginosa

Symptoms of infected mushrooms include bent stems surrounded by mycelium overgrowth at the base. Internally, the roots have linear, water-soaked lines. The caps are twisted, the dwarf. Tissues are spongy and brittle (mummified). Sanitation and the elimination of free water are prevention mechanisms.

Wet Bubble - Mycogone perniciosa

Symptoms include malformed mushrooms with bloated stalks and reduced or deformed tops. Undifferentiated tissue is necrotic and a damp, rot with an unpleasant smell can result. An orange color appears on contaminated mushrooms. Bubbles may be as big as grapefruit. The infection is transmitted by airborne particles and infected containers. It's also a wild mushroom parasite. Controls include irrigation and the use of the compound Sporogone in some countries, which is also very effective against Verticillium.

Dry Bubble - Verticillium

This disease is caused by Verticillium, a fungus that produces sticky spores.

The symptoms created differ with the stage of development of the mushroom at the time of infection. 'Early' pin head contamination results in the development of malformed pinheads, which turn gray / brown and remain leathery. Infection at a later stage causes a thickening of the stem, particularly at the root, as well as a crooked mushroom with a tilted cap and back peeling stalk. Cap infection may occur at a very late stage in the growth of the mushroom, resulting in circular surface spots, initially light brown in color, which becomes gray with age. Verticilium sp. It is possible in soils that may be the main cause of infection, but it is more likely that they may arrive with a coating or by the movement of infection from house to house through pickers, flies, or machines. Spores can lie dormant until they come into contact with mycelium mushroom, which stimulates them to expand. If the spores are oily, the fungus spreads to the dust particles from the earth's movement or to the discarded compost. This dust can contaminate the fresh packaging, or it can penetrate through ventilators or doorways, or it can be brought in by flies, pickers, or even mites. The bacteria inside the processing house can be transmitted by a spill of water. Spores may also be spread to any other equipment used in an infected growing house. The presence of pin head disease indicates infection at an early stage of development, possibly at the time of the incubation. The emergence of the disease at later stages of the production cycle usually indicates that transmission has arisen from other farmhouses or from outside sources. Spreading by wind, flies, and pickers will lead to 30 per cent of the crop becoming polluted by the third flush and the last flush, nearly all of the crop. To regulate Verticillium, the highest standards of hygiene are important. Other monitoring mechanisms are as follows:

Control:

1. Avoid moving the soil near the mushroom houses, particularly on windy days. Take steps to prevent the build-up of dust in the vicinity of the mushroom houses and even the flow of dust in the vicinity of the mushroom houses.
2. Control of flies is necessary, and every effort should be made to prevent them from reaching the farmhouses.
3. When diseased mushrooms emerge, a cloth or a sponge soaked in a disinfectant should be taken from the beds and then put in a bucket containing a disinfectant.

4. Table salt on top of tissue paper may be used to prevent illness.

Fungus gnats (Sciarids)-(Lycoriella spp.) and phorides (Megaselia spp.) Males are tiny (1/8 inch long), delicate, grayish to black, with long, slender legs and thread-like antennas. They have white or smoky-colored wings with no pattern and few distinct veins. The larvae are transparent to creamy-white and can grow to about 1/4 inch in length.

They've got shiny black head capsules. They are drawn to the mushroom flower, and their larvae feed directly on mycelium, swarm over the mushroom, and tunnel into the developed or developing mushroom. Tissues that are physically damaged by flies are often colonized by bacteria that cause soft rot, exacerbating the problem. Controls include strict sanitation and general agricultural hygiene. The through space, for example, must be airtight. The new air used is filtered. Even a small crack would serve as an entry for the flies. Many farms use sticky tape or some other tool to track communities. Biocontrol using nematodes provides efficient regulation when flies are small in populations. In addition to the damage caused to fly larvae by eating mycelium mushrooms or killing pins, adults also have diseases such as Verticillium, Cobwell, and Mycogone.

Mites

Many mites are mostly found in straw and manure, most of which are beneficial to the growth of mushrooms because they feed on eelworms and other mites, but some may cause harm.

Mites, like fly larvae, can feed on mycelium mushrooms and mushrooms where they can induce surface discoloration. They can also exist on other fungi (weeds and indicator molds) used in the cultivation of mushrooms. One example of this is red pepper or pygmy mite (Pymephorus spp.). These mites are commonly associated with the Penicillium and Trichoderma molds on which they feed. Pygmy mites don't feed on Agaricus. These mites have the ability to move to an intermediate stage called a hypopus, where they develop flattened bodies and a sucker plate in which they attach to moving objects, like flies. At this point, the mites swarm on top of the mushrooms.

1. Tarsonemid mite

These mites are light brown and are so small that they can only be observed with the aid of a microscope.

They do harm by feeding the entire hyphae of the mushrooms, and the grower will know if these mites are present, because the base of the mushroom stem will have a reddish-brown discoloration. Where serious infestations occur, the whole base of the mushroom may be removed from the growing surface.

Control

1. As with eelworms, nothing can be done while mites are present in the developing room, so adequate composting and peak heating must be performed to ensure that they are destroyed during the pasteurization process.
2. Good hygiene should be exercised throughout the plant, in particular in the cleaning of crop debris.

2. Tyroglyphic mites (Tyrophagus spp)

These mites can be classified as slow-moving, transparent, with long hairs on their bodies.

If these mites are present in excess, they can eat small pits in the caps and stalks. These pits are then destroyed by bacterial decomposition, which breaks down tissues just below the surface. This ends in the skin melting, leaving the pit exposed. Tyroglyphs may also feed on mycelium mushrooms, where they are present in large numbers, crop declines may be caused.

The mites usually gain entrance into the compost by sticking to the Sciarid flies when the mites are migrating.

Normally, these migratory stages are created when mites are overcrowded.

Mites should not be a concern where there is efficient composting and peak heating. Organic debris should not be allowed to collect around the farm because it provides a breeding ground for mites.

3. Red Pepper Mites (Pygmephorous spp)

These mites are not known to be main pests; their appearance is usually an indicator of the presence of Trichoderma (green mould) in the compost. These mites feed on various plant molds but not on mushrooms, so their appearance means that the compost is unsatisfactory.

The mites are yellowish-brown in color, 0.25 mm in length and have a rounded appearance, and are capable of rapid replication.

As already mentioned, these mites are secondary pets and often swarm on the surfaces of the casings and mushrooms. When this occurs, their presence makes the mushrooms unsaleable. These mites can also disperse Trichoderma spores from bag to bag.

Nematodes-Aphlelenchoides composticola and Ditylenchus myceliophagus These nematodes are widespread in most agricultural soils. Symptoms include mycelium degeneration of mushrooms and the inability to form mushrooms. Normally, an infestation happens at the time of the third split. Mycelium is completely lost in the infected areas, and, as the compost decomposes, it turns black, and the medicinal scent is noticeable. The primary regulation is successful in Phase II.

Abnormalities

Several diseases are of abiotic origin. Popular ones include:

Browning-tyrosinase (phenolase)-is the main enzyme responsible for browning in Agaricus. Calcium chloride in irrigation water prevents bruising by increasing the integrity of the vacuole membranes (thus tyrosinase is not released).

Hard cap, flock, and loose scarf – Anatomical malformation of the hat and gill tissue. Cap is starting early. Causes include certain tumors, toxic pollutants, and genetic anomalies. Hollow-core and brown pit-related to water heat, although not very clear to the exact causes. Big stalks and tiny caps – not enough light and/or fresh air.

Rosecomb-A disease, in which the pink gill tissue, often with a porous texture, grows on the surface of the mushroom cap. The origin was due to pollution from petroleum-based products.

Scaling — The natural reaction of mushrooms cap to dry air.

Stroma-Dight mycelial growth without fruiting. Stroma happens when the spawn is mishandled or exposed to harmful petroleum-based gasses or chemicals. It can also be used in dry environments.

Weepers-The mushroom is spilling water out of the tip. The root is not known but can be found in low-moisture compost and high-moisture casings.

CHAPTER SIX

Foraging: Identifying Magic Mushrooms And The Benefits Of Psilocybin

Destroying Angel (Amanita virosa), tasty Caesar fungus (Amanita caesera), and hallucinogenic Fly Amanita or toadstool (Amanita muscaria). How do you know which one of these you've just come across?

A mushroom guide is a must for those interested in foraging mushrooms. It's good if the guide contains photos of toxic mushrooms, but because of the sheer amount of options, it's much more useful if the guide will provide nothing on the fungus when you insert details on the specimen you've discovered. One such mushroom guide, published by researchers at the University of Aarhus and the University of Copenhagen, Denmark, is available online. It's called MycoKey, though there are other similar references out there as well.

A variety of variables are used in a correct identification. It requires not only size, but also location, season, and growing conditions. However, if you cannot make a definitive diagnosis, certain general characteristics can alert you to the possibility of a dangerous species.

Neither Plant Nor Animal

A mushroom appears to grow like a plant, but it's not a plant. Genetically, the bodies of the fungus are similar to those of the mammals, but the fungus is not an insect itself. It is a mushroom. In addition, a mushroom is not something that grows independently. It's just the fruiting portion of a secret creature called mycelium. Mycelium is a weblike structure that grows underground or within the rotting wood pores and can grow very large. There is a mycelium in the Blue Mountains of California which has reached 2.4 miles long and is perhaps the largest living creature on Earth.

Thanks to the right conditions and ample moisture, mycelium sprouts its fruiting bodies, which pierce the surface of the developing medium and develop into structures characteristic of the genus. Structures vary, but usually contain the following components: cap – this may be parasol-shaped or cup-shaped, conical or oval, and may be mottled, smooth or filled with small nibs. It may or may not have skin that is easy to strip down.

Seed – The seed goes from the cap to the growing source. This may be long and slim or short and heavy. Not all of the mushrooms have a stem. Many that grow on decayed wood don't but appear more as puffballs that are huge, round and often edible (though some poisonous mushrooms look like puffballs when they're smaller, so you can't say that the puffy stuff on the ground is safe to eat).

The gills are the spore-producing part of mushrooms. They are usually on the underside of the cap, which may be ribbed or made up of a wide number of small holes. Many mushrooms have protuberances called teeth instead of gills, and others, such as chanterelles, have veins.

Ring or Annulus – When the ring is present, it is usually wound around the stem just below the tip. It's a reminder of the ubiquitous curtain that the fungus needed to crack through when it sprouted.

Volva – Volva is a bulging part of the base of the stem. The feature cannot be seen above the ground. The existance of a volva, particularly one with a ring around it, is always a sign that the species is poisonous.

Two Tips To Help With The Identification Of Poisonous Mushroom

Once you encounter a fungus, a few defining characteristics will help you identify the propensity for a fungus to be poisonous. These are not convincing in the sense that many edible species show these characteristics, but if you consider them, they are a good indication that you should leave the mushroom alone. You could miss out on a delicious treat, but more importantly, you're not going to die. And do not make a mistake: death is a real possibility. Approximately 60% of cases involving Amanita and other animals result in death. The guidelines are as follows: white gill mushrooms are poisonous, as are those with a ring around the band or volva. Since the volva is always underground, it is important to dig around the base of the mushroom to reach it.

Mushrooms with a red dye on the cap or stem are also either poisonous or extremely hallucinogenic. The most common red mushroom is Amanita muscaria, which has been used to induce hallucinations for thousands of years. Even this "rust fungus" can be deadly in large doses. Many Amanita species, too, have this coloring and are much less benign.

Guidelines for Toxic Mushroom Identification

The consequences of misidentifying a mushroom can be severe, so it is important to ask yourself some important questions before you harvest one that you have come across. Where's the mushroom growing? If it's under a vine, what kind of vine is it? If it grows on wood, what kind of tree is it? For example, hen of the woods mushrooms are generally harmless – even medicinal – but they have the ability to make you sick if they grow on conifers, eucalyptus, or cedar trees. Also note if the mushroom grows on its own or in a circle, in the sun or shade, and at what time of year it is.

When you feel confident enough to handle your mushroom – preferably with gloves – you can measure the gills, check the rings, and look for a volva. Move the cap or use a knife to make a small slit. Does the cap change color, and if so, what color does it change into? You could also cut a small piece off and sniff it. Poisonous mushrooms often have an unpleasant, acrid smell. You can also get the specifics by cutting the stem and sticking the cap on a piece of paper, gill-side down for a few hours to print the spore. A white spore print is a telling sign of the genus Amanita.

Using an Online Mushroom Guide

It's worth repeating the warning that you should never eat a mushroom unless you can positively identify it. The use of an online catalog is a simple way to achieve positive identification. You can recognize a harmful fungus by looking at pictures of poisonous mushrooms, but if you can't find any of the one you're looking for, go to a site that allows you to enter the specifics of the specimen. Usually, the search begins with the general shape of the specimen and its gill structure, followed by specifics such as cap and gill color and texture, height, and growing conditions. When you have learned the genus and the species, you can see information about the edibility – or lack there of – of the organism.

Remember that mushrooms can be both deceptively attractive and deadly. The aptly called Destroying Angel is a perfect example of that. Dangerous mushrooms may also look like benign ones. For example, the sprout of Amanita looks like a young buffalo, so you can't tell the difference unless you pierce the veil and look for gills inside, which means that the specimen is possibly poisonous. If you're not certain about that, just leave the mushroom alone.

Wild psilocybin mushrooms are found in a variety of places across the globe and grow in at least ten distinct varieties. Psilocybe cubensis, the most common psilocybin-containing wild mushroom, is found in the United States, Mexico, Central, and South America and the West Indies. Psilocybe cubensis, the most common psilocybin-containing wild mushroom, has not yet been identified as a strain. Psilocybin mushrooms can also be known by their size, shape, and stem swelling, which produces a blue shade.

Young Psilocybe cubensis mushrooms (usually smaller ones) can have a dark golden brown color, whereas more mature ones have a light golden brown color.

Test the mushroom stem and see if it has a blue tint. This color, which may be caused by the mixture of oxygen and psilocybin, occurs with swelling of any sort. If a human, mosquito, or even grass or other mushroom has touched a mushroom, this reaction is likely to occur.

You're looking for a dark purple gill coat. This mushroom veil is a very thin layer that persists on the gills of the mushroom until the mushroom cap is fully expanded, at which point it splits. Sometimes a split veil can be seen around the stems of psilocybin mushrooms.

Psychedelics Could Be Next Breakthrough Treatment

Experts suggest the safe medicinal "magic mushrooms" have multiple possible benefits from treating addiction to help manage alcohol dependency.

Soft lighting. Comfortable furniture. Tasteful decoration of the walls. This setting seems like it's a dining room to the untrained eye. But in fact it is a research laboratory specifically designed to evoke comfort and ease. A session of psilocybin therapy is occurring here.

On the couch lies a patient. He is wearing an eye mask and headphones. Gentle music is going to be played. Two members of the research team are available to help direct the 8-hour session. The bulk of this time is spent in quiet introspection. Skilled emergency personnel are on-site if anything happens suddenly.

This therapy session, amid the trappings of normalcy, is anything but.

Psilocybin is a powerful psychedelic. While it is approximately 100 times less effective than LSD, it is capable of modifying the perception of space and time, inducing sensory hallucinations, euphoria, and spiritual experiences. Unlike weed, which has experienced a drastic change in both legalization interest and accepted medical applications, or MDMA, which has been highlighted in recent years for its ability to treat PTSD (some experts suggest that the medication may be licensed by the Food and Drug Administration as early as 2021), psilocybin lacks the same degree of popular cachet.

And one may be forgiven for speaking of "sheep" as nothing more than a legacy of the psychedelic excesses of the 1960s. Yet don't make a mistake: Psilocybin has a variety of possible health benefits.

The State Of Psilocybin Research

Psilocybin has proven that it has the ability to treat a wide variety of psychological and mental conditions, but in the United States the FDA has not yet approved it for any use.

Its use has had positive outcomes in the treatment of insomnia, obsessive-compulsive disorder, smoking cessation, alcohol dependence, cluster headaches, cocaine addiction, and cancer-related or other end-of-life psychological distress.

Recent high-profile campaigns to decriminalize psilocybin mushrooms have been held in Denver, Colorado, and Oregon. Analysts, however, claim this is unlikely to happen. Psilocybin mushrooms are classified as Schedule I, according to the Drug Enforcement Administration, which means that they are listed as having "no generally approved therapeutic use and a high potential for misuse." Other substances in Schedule I include marijuana, MDMA, and LSD. However, despite its classification and stigma, doctors are undertaking FDA-approved clinical trials.

A non-profit research organization focused on the medicinal applications of psychedelics, in particular psilocybin, explains its motivations: "Our mission is twofold: to do a study that lets us understand the mind, the brain, how all this works, and to help relieve pain through the clinical application of psychedelics." The institute is currently working on two main fields of psilocybin research. Cancer-related psilocybin therapy is known to be one of the most important areas of drug research.

However, given the vast number of potential applications for psilocybin, it is necessary to bear in mind that the amount of analysis also ranges significantly, from single pilot studies to FDA Phase II or III approval testing.

Here's what existing research says about the application of psilocybin.

Depression

Depression is one of the most studied reasons for psilocybin therapy and the findings are promising. The Usona Institute, a psychedelic research center, is currently in the preparation phase of its stage III experiment, which is expected to launch this year.

Smoking cessation and other addictions

In a brief pilot trial at Johns Hopkins University, researchers found that psilocybin treatment substantially enhanced smoking abstinence over a 12-month follow-up span.

Psilocybin also has the ability to cure certain drug use conditions, including alcohol and cocaine dependency.

"The basic theory is that the essence of such diseases is a small emotional and behavioral repertoire. So, [psilocybin] in well-orchestrated sessions [has] the potential to essentially shake someone out of their habit and provide a snapshot of a bigger image and establish emotional plasticity in which people will step outside of these issues." Additionally, a recent open-label analysis on psilocybin and alcohol dependency showed that following therapy both smoking and heavy drinking decreased. Researchers in Alabama are also running psilocybin treatment experiments for drug misuse.

Cancer-related psychiatric trauma

The treatment we have the most data on is for cancer-related depression and anxiety. There have been some positive research findings in areas such as the management of intense suicidal fear in individuals approaching the end of their lives who are diagnosed with advanced cancer.

A professor who is associated with the Heffter Research Institute researched psilocybin extensively and published work on the subject, including a 2011 pilot report on psilocybin anxiety management in people with cancer.

A randomized, double-blind study at Johns Hopkins in 2016 showed that a single dose of psilocybin greatly increased quality of life and reduced depression and anxiety in patients living with life-threatening cancer.

But will psilocybin ever be approved by the FDA? Despite encouraging studies, there is no concrete timetable for whether or not psilocybin will actually be accepted by the FDA. Most experts agree that the drug may be dangerous for a number of reasons if improperly administered. Psilocybin impacts the cardiovascular system and can lead to high blood pressure or erratic heartbeat. It also has the potential to inflict severe and persistent psychiatric issues.

According to some studies, psilocybin is even more clinically harmful than cannabis so it is particularly risky for a small proportion of the population that has experienced an episode of depression or mania, a depressive event, or those who have, perhaps, an immediate family member who has had such issues, as it may induce a psychotic or depressive experience in an individual that is susceptible to it. There are also uncommon but recorded instances of people leaping to their deaths or otherwise acting erratically in a manner that endangers themselves or those around them. Of course, taken under chaotic conditions, all bets are off. You don't know what you're going to get.

However, therapeutic psilocybin treatment is nothing like spontaneously deciding to eat shrooms at a wedding. It is intended to be administered in a carefully managed environment to ensure that nothing unforeseen occur. Any risks can be controlled for and mitigated. There are dangers, but they are significantly minimized under scientific medical administration and possibly in accepted therapeutic practice, and I'd suggest that these hazards and our abilities to handle them are acceptable relative to many of the techniques that are commonly performed in medicine. Although some are hopeful that psilocybin may follow in the footsteps of MDMA treatment and theoretically have clearance in the next 5 to 10 years, the mechanism is far from simple and very unclear. In large part, there hasn't been enough research done to date.

Conclusion

Considering the lack of alternative approaches for researching such compounds, the resurgence of scientific and interdisciplinary research activities is a more critical topic than ever before. Above all, a large number of patients can benefit from a deeper understanding of psychotropic drugs, likely leading to mental and psychological healing processes. A glimmer of optimism for the resurgence of large-scale research emerges from the United Kingdom, where a relatively limited number of scientists have periodically been able to secure federal approval to perform experiments on the therapeutic effects of hallucinogens, including psilocybin. The philosophical framework underlying the creation of these research initiatives indicates that there is practically no credible pharmacological evidence available. In addition, these compounds have undergone comprehensive studies over the course of many decades.

To the degree that dosage and effect correlations have already been established, current and future research activities will draw on existing information instead of neglecting or overlooking previously reported findings. High-tech methods can produce new techniques for exploring and improving our knowledge of biochemical mushrooms. Nevertheless, expanded biochemical awareness does not allow one to draw any conclusions about certain facets of psychoactive drugs such as psychedelic peak encounters or discovering the boundaries of the subconscious mind, nor enable designing medical strategies focused on these effects.

Printed in Great Britain
by Amazon